"Jocelyn's infectious joy and love for food and family leap from the pages to your table. Your family will be begging for seconds in no time."

—JENNIFER GARNER, actor

"To say Jocelyn is one of my favorite food voices is an understatement. Her recipes are beyond delicious and gorgeous, and I've never made a dish of hers that I didn't love and devour. Hands down one of my favorite cookbooks in recent memory!"

—REE DRUMMOND, #1 *New York Times* bestselling author of *The Pioneer Woman Cooks*

"There isn't a cookbook I am more excited about than *Everyday Grand*! The recipes are colorful, full of so much incredible flavor, and simple to make for the everyday home cook. I am so excited to continue to cook through it!"

—TIEGHAN GERARD, founder of *Half Baked Harvest*

"*Everyday Grand* is like having a slice of sunshine on your bookshelf. It radiates joy, love, and the promise of good times for friends and family."

—AL ROKER, feature and weather anchor on *Today,* cohost on *3rd Hour Today*

"*Everyday Grand* is worth your time in so many ways. This is a tasty invitation to thrive and dine with generations of Jocelyn's family."

—SUNNY ANDERSON, Food Network host, *New York Times* bestselling author of *Sunny's Kitchen: Easy Food for Real Life*

"Jocelyn can make anything taste grand. From her delectable desserts to her savory Southern dishes, I can't wait to cook through all these amazing recipes with my own family."

—TIFFANI THIESSEN, actor, producer, and author

"Jocelyn incorporates family into every meal, offering a fresh take on all the favorites you grew up with, including new, delicious additions!"

—KATHERINE SCHWARZENEGGER PRATT, *New York Times* bestselling author

"Filled with delicious, approachable recipes, this book exudes a sense of joy and celebration and includes Southern favorites you'll be making over and over."

—JOHN KANELL, founder of *Preppykitchen*

"This cookbook highlights Jocelyn's positivity, reminding us to celebrate moments both big and small. I can't wait to make so many recipes, starting with Auntie's Southern Baked Chicken!"

—GINA HOMOLKA, author of *The SkinnyTaste Cookbook*

"Adams isn't just an amazing home cook, she's a spark of joy and light that everyone is drawn to. I love how much her personality comes through in every page."

—DEB PERELMAN, author of *Smitten Kitchen Keepers*

Everyday GRAND

Soulful Recipes

FOR CELEBRATING LIFE'S BIG AND SMALL MOMENTS

Jocelyn Delk Adams

WITH OLGA MASSOV

PHOTOGRAPHS BY BRITTANY CONERLY

CLARKSON POTTER/PUBLISHERS
NEW YORK

*To my daughter,
Harmony, who gives
me reasons to celebrate
every single day*

Happiness isn't always an indication that everything in your life is perfect, or that things are necessarily flowing your way. Sometimes, happiness is simply the choice to see the light in everything that you can, despite how imperfect or unclear your current situation may be. —BILLY CHAPATA

contents

let's celebrate!

"Thank you, God, for waking me up this morning." This is a popular Black Christian adage that I say to myself every day and have heard in probably every church service I've ever attended. The simple act of breathing is truly a blessing, and it's the most basic thing we should be grateful for. If you are breathing, it's reason enough to celebrate.

Most people tend to focus on major events and holidays: birthdays, anniversaries, Christmas, Thanksgiving, Passover, Ramadan. But what else deserves to be celebrated? In my world, anything and everything. In between those big events are life's little moments, and they, too, are bursting with joy. When my daughter took her first steps, I baked a cake. When I finally finished reading a book that was on my to-do list for over a year, I threw a batch of cookies in the oven. When my favorite show returned after a long hiatus, I cooked the most epic dinner. I've found that surprising your loved ones or friends with a mini celebration of LIFE is always more fun than expected.

The seed for this book may have been originally planted by my grandmother Maggie Small. Big Mama, as we used to call her, celebrated two birthdays. While she had a birth certificate with a specific birthdate, she insisted the date was wrong. And so we celebrated twice, on August 6 and August 13—the date she thought was the right one and the date on the birth certificate. The joy Big Mama had, and her desire to celebrate more—not less—is a lesson we can all learn from. (Inspired by her, I've really

run with the birthday concept and now celebrate my whole birthday *month*, because why not?)

Most of our lives are made up of small moments, and those moments can bring us so much more joy when we take time to appreciate and acknowledge them. We all know the stress that comes with the big holidays, when stores build their displays and try to convince us that happiness and fulfillment lie in a gift. But this is different. What happens in between those big calendar events is the everyday life we live—the glorious, messy, filled-with-tiny-moments life—that is also worth appreciating. Are you having a good hair day? Celebrate! Did you just cross something off your bucket list? Let's toast! Did your pet have a birthday? If that's not an excuse for cake, what is? Honoring *those* moments with a pressure-free dinner or dessert can create memories that last a lifetime.

> *Are you having a good hair day? Celebrate!*

In the spirit of this mindful shift to celebrating life and cultivating joy, I also want this book to honor the African American experience. Part of Black survival is learning to laugh, dance, and smile through the most painful and troubling moments. From slavery to segregation to Jim Crow laws to the civil rights and BLM movements—these experiences have steeled us into a people of resilience, strength, and power. Even our homegoings (funerals), despite the somber occasion, are filled with celebration and gratitude as we come together and remember the life of the deceased. Our joy truly comes from within, because even our everyday experiences are cloaked in being Black. Finding joy even amid pain or monotony is the way we get through things. It's our survival mechanism. We can form a *Soul Train* line or do the Wobble anywhere—and everywhere.

My appreciation for life's small moments was a gradual shift that took place over time. The birth of my daughter, Harmony, made me take stock of what I considered a priority. Watching her grow and change was a celebration in and of itself. First smile, first word, first steps—these moments were as important as any holiday I've ever observed. I started to search for more meaning and joy in everyday things. I started questioning some practices we hold sacrosanct: We keep these insanely long to-do lists and work ourselves into a frenzy, and where does it get us? I had been running on autopilot for too long.

As I started to settle into my new routine, I began to discover joy in the moments I was building rituals around: writing in my journal, creating a meditation practice, putting a pause on social media—even though my profession depends on it. When I started to spend less time online, I became much more present in the here and now.

Then the 2020 COVID-19 pandemic hit, and everyone's lives changed overnight. Get-togethers, vacations, social plans were all put on hold—indefinitely. We had to relearn how to live with the people in our homes. Whereas I once saw my husband for just a few hours every morning and evening, now I was seeing him around the clock, along with my mother and father, with whom we were living as we waited for our new house to be built. We were cooking three meals a day for days, weeks, and months. Date nights out were replaced by date nights in, sandwiched between folding the laundry and putting Harmony to sleep.

Since we weren't leaving our homes much, we were forced to find joyful moments in the everyday things—and in one another. Our typical holiday family gatherings became smaller, quieter affairs, with just the people living in the household. As I let it sink in how different it all looked, I began to redefine what constitutes a celebration. It dawned on me that all moments, as many as possible, in fact, needed to be celebrated—and not just during the pandemic, but beyond it.

You might have heard the saying "When God closes the door, He opens a window." Perhaps the silver lining of the close living forced on us by COVID was taking a step back, shifting our perspectives, and reevaluating what is truly important to us. What happens when the ground shakes beneath us? When the world—and life as you know it—shifts, can you shift with it?

What I think of as a celebration has changed. Really, sitting in this moment has become more important to me. There's always been, for me, the chase of accomplishment, but its importance has paled. Do I want to be answering a million emails when my daughter is playing in the other room and I could be with her instead? I don't want to miss these fleeting moments. And maybe instead of creating another Instagram Reel, I'll use my phone to call a relative, record my family history, and capture my heritage as I learn about my family tree. I don't want to let the wonderful moments in my life pass by and go unacknowledged.

Life isn't a string of holidays we move from and to. Acing a test, getting that job offer, finally finishing a book you've been reading for a while should be just as much cause for joy as a wedding anniversary or holiday. We should celebrate our *real* lives. And the more we try to take the time to do so, the more purposeful and joyful our lives will feel.

Take stock in your everyday accomplishments: They matter. You matter.

Take stock in your everyday accomplishments: They matter. You matter. No thing, regardless of how seemingly insignificant, isn't worth celebrating: Your child losing their first tooth, your pet learning a new trick, paying off that credit card balance, or making your bed several days in a row. Keeping a plant alive longer than you thought you could. Sorting through a pile of mail. Smiling to yourself first thing in the morning. It's all worthy of acknowledgment.

And this is where my book comes in. I'm not suggesting it's a shortcut to joy—that work needs to be done by you and you alone—but it can be a bridge to that place where you become content from within, delighted and grateful for each day, each moment, taking in your blessings. And what better way to honor it all than by cooking and sharing that joy with others? These recipes and stories, full of comfort and inspiration, are just a jumping-off point—where you take your own journey of giving thanks for your everyday accomplishments and victories is truly up to you, be it cornmeal biscuits à la Big Mama (page 30) or a Cajun lobster roll (page 153) or even your own Italian herb-and-spice blend (page 64). You write the blueprint for your life, and you get to erect and furnish that edifice with the events, people, and, yes, foods that bring you the utmost joy. I'm truly honored to come with you on this journey.

So, let's celebrate—together.

celebrate good times

A cause for celebration, to me, can be as small as a good hair day or as big as an actual holiday, or a gathering like my family's annual fish fry or Big Mama's two birthdays. Below are some ideas, and if you need a jumping-off point for menus for these and other celebrations, check out page 250.

Juneteenth

Martin Luther King Jr. Day

Family reunions

HBCU homecoming and its significance

Crossing something off your bucket list

Following your passion

Falling in love

Your child taking their first steps, saying their first words, etc.

Treat Yo' Self Day

Creating a healthier you!

Finishing that book you've been "meaning to get to"

Friday (the end of a long workweek)

Learning a new hobby

A warm, sunny day

Sunday supper

Simple gratitude days

Game days

Netflix-and-chill nights

Becoming inspired by something new!

Picnic

Self-care day

Cancer in remission

Solo days (go to the movies by yourself, cook a meal you love, embrace being with and enjoying that time with yourself)

Overcoming a fear

Paying off that last student loan!

Planning a vacation

Saying "yes" to a new opportunity

Kwanzaa

National Popcorn Day (January 19), Proposal Day (March 10), Siblings Day (April 10), Ice Cream Day (July 17), Watermelon Day (August 3), Soup Day (November 19), Fritter Day (December 2)

Surprise Valentine's Day (choose a day on the calendar and surprise your partner—romance!)

Birthday week/month

A streak of consistent exercising

Completing your first race

recipes for joy

"Joy is a conscious daily choice that comes from within.
No one else can create your joy—or change it."

My goal for this book is to invite you to my idea of the ultimate family reunion, a supreme gathering of folks in the Black community. Elevated energy, laughter, pure joy, brilliant conversation, amazing food, and lively experiences. I want reading and cooking from this book to feel like the moment you get a hug from a cousin you haven't seen in a while, or when you hear Frankie Beverly & Maze on the radio. Happiness. Bliss. A true celebration of what it means to live in a state of joy and experience the food that makes your soul smile.

Remember: Joy is a conscious daily choice that comes from within. No one else can create your joy—or change it. Every single day I boldly choose joy! It is a mantra I recite to myself, and I want you to choose it for yourself as well.

I hope the stories and suggested celebrations in this book will encourage you to find moments throughout the day to breathe in and out and return to the present. Dedicating time to meditate and silence your mind is crucial to peace. Embrace this moment right here, right now.

I have found that meals are a wonderful way to prioritize being present while nurturing relationships that are important to you, whether they are for hard conversations that settle arguments and create peace, or just for gathering with loved ones to catch up. Meals are also a wonderful way to give: to build new friendships, welcome a neighbor, nourish new parents, comfort those experiencing a loss, or celebrate a big or small win.

In this book, you'll find some recipes that are unchanged from how my Big Mama made them, because I believe the simplicity of their ingredients and approach should be preserved. I hope to continue amplifying the voices of those who came before me, because the food I make now wouldn't exist without what I experienced before. You'll also find my wacky, fun, and experimental vibez in these recipes. Some folks are worried that by delving into new dishes and food experiences, they will lose touch with their own culinary history and what they were taught about food and community. For me, honoring recipes that came before me is just as important as striking out to create my own culinary language. Both can coexist—the old and the new. My hope is that the recipes I've shared with you in the pages that follow will ignite creativity in the kitchen, drop flavor bombs on your taste buds, and inspire conversations at the dinner table. My goal was to create a collection of recipes for everyone and for every kind of celebration, especially the everyday events that may get overlooked.

I don't believe in bougie food; if a food experience makes me feel "less than" or gives pompous, pretentious BS, I'm not here for it. Food should comfort and make

everyone feel welcome at the table. Sure, techniques vary, but I know for a fact that while I've been blessed to experience food in high-end restaurants from Paris and Barcelona to Ireland and Mexico, some of the best meals I've ever had were made by somebody's grandmama in a small market stall, no table settings or wine pairings required. Their soul was there, and it made all the difference.

Take time to understand how food transcends its creation: It can take on new possibilities and honor the past in a way many things don't. Recipes are not just instructions for cooking—they are also narratives, experiences, and pieces of history. Recipes are a chronicle of time where the past, present, and future come together. By re-creating our family recipes, we honor those who came before us by giving their legacy a new life and lay the foundation for future generations to know their origins and establish traditions of their own.

So pull up a chair and have a seat at my table. I'm so glad to have you here.

7 lists of 7 life and kitchen essentials

Seven might be a lucky number for many, but it has deep personal meaning for me. It's the day of my birthday and the day my baby girl, Harmony, my biggest blessing, entered this world (June 7 and February 7, respectively). Harmony was also two weeks late (like mother, like daughter), as God decided we were both to be born on the seventh day of the month. We will always be connected by this number. So in honor of this incredibly meaningful number in my life, here are seven lists of my life and kitchen essentials.

When I wake up in the morning, I'm always tempted to reach for my phone first, but instead I allow myself time to breathe in and out, take in my surroundings, and contemplate my blessings. In general, if I had to choose one nugget of wisdom to share with y'all, it would be to be more present in the real world than the social media one. Facebook ain't real, boos! While you're wishing for the seeming perfection of someone's curated feed, you're missing out on real life. So put that phone down. Get off TikTok during dinner; set a time each evening when you shut your phone off until the next day—and take in all the things that make your life truly beautiful.

These are my go-to affirmations—they help me move through the day with more gratitude, purpose, and intention.

1 Today is filled with so much promise and beauty. Today, I am not my past and can create my own future. The sky's the limit on today's possibilities. Limitations do not exist.

2 I express gratitude today. I'm grateful for the opportunity to grow and share my love, gifts, and joy today. I will laugh today and every day. I will find my inner child today. The biggest wins in my life happen when I'm happy.

3 I will protect my energy and prioritize myself and the energy I put out there. I will try to stay in a high vibrational state of energy—energy that is good, strong, positive, and uplifting, because it always begets blessings.

4 Nourishing my mind is just as important as nourishing my body. Everything just hits differently when both are in alignment. I will look at life through a lens of positivity and surround myself with generous, gracious, giving people who will support and nurture me as I support and nurture myself.

5 Remember that abundance is more than wealth. I create an abundance of clarity. Abundance of peace. Abundance of joy. Abundance of blessings.

6 Self-care is not a self-serving act: Just as I'm instructed on an airplane to first put on my own mask before assisting others, I must remember that I cannot truly help those around me if I'm not really taking care of myself. I'm allowed to claim and schedule rest for myself, and it's okay for me to say no, if it doesn't align with my spirit.

7 I will not compare myself to others. I will remember my worth and stand strong in knowing it. My path is my own; I'm unique and cannot be replaced or replicated. I will remember that knowing my worth means never negotiating who I am.

1 a cast-iron skillet—or five

If your space doesn't allow for it, I recommend a minimum of two skillets: a 9-inch one and a 12-inch one. They will take you from medium-size dishes to roasting a chicken. While many home cooks are afraid of cast iron, it's actually pretty low maintenance. Some hot water and a nice scrub are all you need (maybe salt sometimes to get rid of extra stuck-on bits). Don't wash a cast-iron pan with soap or stick it in the dishwasher. Don't leave it in your sink overnight covered with water. Just wash, dry quickly over a flame, and wipe clean. Some folks swear by reseasoning their cast iron from time to time, but if y'all are treating your skillet right, it'll renew that seasoning on its own and keep getting better and better the more you use it. If you didn't inherit a vintage cast-iron pan like I did, I recommend looking for one at estate sales or yard sales—they are unmatched in quality and are lighter than modern-day versions. If you'd prefer a brand-new skillet, Lodge makes affordable ones. If you take good care of it, it will last you a lifetime, and you can pass it on to your grandbabies, if you'd like.

P.S. A quality cast-iron Dutch oven, often coated with a layer of beautiful enamel, is also a must-have. I use mine for braised meats, roasts, soups, stews, and even deep-frying. You can go high-end and get a Staub or Le Creuset Dutch oven, which will last a lifetime, or opt for an inexpensive version by Lodge, which will do the work admirably.

2 big mama's collection of old handwritten recipes and cookbooks

When I'm cooking and baking, especially from Big Mama's recipes and cookbooks, I feel her spirit in the kitchen with me. These micro-records of history are a way for me to feel connected to her and channel what she herself experienced when she opened those books and prepared those recipes. Making those dishes inspires me in new ways because they are truly the blueprint for how a lot of Southern Black recipes evolved and took shape. Learning the traditional ways foods were cooked and the roots of how recipes were developed when resources were limited is also immensely inspiring. If you haven't inherited cookbooks like these, try browsing your local thrift stores and used book shops—I've been able to find some of the most incredible vintage cookbooks while thrifting. I also suggest creating your own generational cookbooks to pass down in the future.

3 digital scale

Weighing your ingredients, especially in metric measures (grams), arms you with greater accuracy in your measurements, which is especially important in baking—and particularly critical if you find baking intimidating. You'll discover that all the baking recipes in this book include metric weight measurements for ingredients. Scooping up a cup of flour, depending on how you dip the scoop and if your flour is compacted, will give you anywhere from 120 to 150 grams. These differences add up if you're using more than a cup of flour in a recipe and will definitely affect the outcome. But 125 grams is 125 grams no matter how you slice it. So, boos, get yourselves a scale. They ain't expensive—around $20 is all you need to spend. And I promise you this much: A kitchen scale will not only change *how* you cook but will also make you a much more *successful* cook. In fact, you may look back on your scale-less past and not comprehend how you got on without it.

4 bomb chef's knives

A high-quality, sharp, easy-to-maneuver chef's knife is essential to prepping in the kitchen. I suggest going to a great kitchen store so you can pick up the knives and find one that feels good in your hand. Get a sense of how a knife feels before purchasing it, since high-quality knives can be a bit pricey. I personally love my 8-inch Shun chef's knife. To round out the collection, I have a small, cheap paring knife and a good serrated bread knife. Those three knives are pretty much all you need to get by in the kitchen.

5 bench scraper

From perfectly frosting my cakes to cutting dough to scraping stuck-on batter off the counter, this inexpensive tool is crucial in my kitchen. I have both a short one and a long one. They replace my knives when I'm working with pastry and are also fantastic for scraping and gathering ingredients to transfer to a skillet or pan. King Arthur and OXO make bench scrapers that will last you a long time and won't break the bank. If you like one with a wooden handle (it sure looks fly on the counter), don't stick it in the dishwasher, or the wood will eventually warp and split.

6 instant-read thermometer

From making my Mojito-Marinated Skirt Steak with Chimichurri (page 168) to my Blood Orange Caramels (page 217), this is a crucial tool in my arsenal, because overcooking or undercooking can be a death sentence to a recipe. I love my ThermoWorks Thermapen, which is a little pricey, but their less expensive ThermoPop is also very good.

7 baking sheet

What would I do without a baking sheet—or several? It is such a crucial and handy tool for making everything from Roasted Mango, Sweet Potato, and Butternut Squash (page 124) and French Onion Sheet Pan Chicken (page 187) to My Favorite Salted Caramel Chocolate Chip Cookies (page 214) during the holiday season. Baking sheets stack nicely and take up little space even in the most cramped kitchens. They also double well as trays for carrying ingredients out to the grill or even organizing ingredients in your pantry. I don't believe in spending a whole bunch of money on these, but a decent one made from high-quality aluminum will ensure everything bakes a bit more evenly. Nordic Ware and Chicago Metallic are good, reliable, inexpensive brands.

1 hot sauce

I got hot sauce in my (pantry) swag bag! I bring on as much spice as humanly possible, and you may find that some of my recipes pack serious heat. If Nashville Hot were a person, it would be me. My fam's hot sauce of choice is Louisiana, but I keep Tabasco, sriracha, Frank's RedHot, and sambal oelek on hand as well.

2 self-rising flour

I try to stock self-rising flour in addition to all-purpose flour—my Big Mama swore by the White Lily and Martha White brands, especially for biscuits. It helps to produce the most tender and flaky biscuits and is worth seeking out.

3 apple cider vinegar

I find that the flavor of apple cider vinegar complements many of my recipes. I always grab the Bragg brand, which is an organic raw vinegar and comes with the "mother."

4 worcestershire sauce

You may be super surprised to find a lot of my recipes use Worcestershire, and there's a reason for it: It is so damn good! The sauce takes something from good to explosive with just a dash of its concentrated potency. I use Worcestershire in gravies, marinades, and sauces to perk up dishes in an unexpected way. There are also some great gluten-free and vegan varieties on the market.

5 canned chipotle peppers in adobo sauce

Chipotles in adobo are my jam, and I use them for many recipes outside my fave Mexican-inspired fare. I use both the chipotles and the adobo sauce. Y'all, I throw these babies in my marinades for fried chicken to really amp up the flavor. Sometimes I'll even randomly puree one and add it to a sauce just because I can—it's my world! And I'm giving you permission to do this, too. Roll the dice a bit.

6 tamari

When I realized that some of my family had gluten sensitivities, I swapped my beloved soy sauce for tamari and haven't looked back. Tamari is also made from soy, but doesn't include wheat like soy sauce does, so there's no gluten. It still gives that distinct and strong umami flavor that can take a dish over the edge.

7 grits

Saved the best for last, y'all! The beauty and pride of the Black struggle can be largely found in our culinary identity. Before it became hot in the streets to eat "our" foods, they were simple reflections of our everyday lives. Grits weren't the $20 delicacy we now see on the menus of popular Southern-inspired restaurants in major cities—they were a dish I ate almost every day. We don't play around with instant grits, either—grits need time and patience. I personally love a medium grind, but I also like the texture of stone-ground grits.

1 butter

Here's the thing: If it were up to me, my fridge would actually consist of all butter (with maybe a bottle of water here and there), because that's how essential it is to me. You know those people who buy one pack of butter and that lasts them for weeks? That ain't me. I am most secure when there are at least four of those boxes between my fridge and my freezer. I start getting a bit anxious when that number falls below three. From Auntie's Southern Baked Chicken (page 184) to my winning carrot cake (page 211) and Blood Orange Caramels (page 217), butter is nonnegotiable. I always keep unsalted *and* salted versions in the fridge and sometimes stock higher-fat European options when I wanna get supa classy, ya dig?

2 garlic

Garlic makes everything taste better. The more the merrier. I believe in loads of it, and add cloves upon cloves because it is a flavor bomb. When looking for garlic in the grocery store or at the farmers' market, hold a head of it in your hand; it should feel dense and slightly heavy for its size. If it feels like it's filled with air, the cloves are dried out and the garlic won't be good.

3 eggs

Eggs make the world go 'round. I use them equally in baking and cooking. They bind ingredients together, add structure and stability to baked goods, and, when used as egg wash, help create that beautiful burnished look. I also love me a good egg for breakfast, like my jambalaya frittata (page 36).

4 lemons

If I could write a love letter to lemons, I would, boos. I start every day with a warm glass of water with fresh lemon juice. A naturopath recommended this to me years ago, and I haven't looked back. The lemon water hydrates and energizes you, and also gives your digestive system a wake-up call when it wants to hit the snooze button. I find that lemon juice and zest brighten recipes and enliven ingredients in such a special way, and the acid can give a recipe the kick in the ass it needs to fully reach its potential. That's probably why I love lemon pepper so much, too!

5 buttermilk

Buttermilk is the MVP for a lot of recipes in this book. My Cereal-Crusted Buffalo Chicken Tenders (page 61) and Hot Sauce–Chipotle Fried Chicken (page 189) find their thick buttermilk dip or bath essential for imparting tenderness, extra tang, flavor, and richness. And buttermilk gives you that almost buttery flavor you won't find in just plain ol' whole milk. I love to use it in my cornbread and biscuits for the same reason. It is time we give buttermilk her flowers. If you don't want to keep it around, since it's a specialty grocery item for many folks, simply make a pretty good dupe by stirring 1 teaspoon of my beloved lemon juice or white vinegar into 1 cup of whole milk and letting it sit for about 10 minutes, until it sours and thickens. But just know that buttermilk lasts for months in the fridge, so it's worth having on hand. Worst case, you can add it to your milkshake and bring all the boys to the yard.

6 ginger

Fresh ginger has found a way into my kitchen like none other. Every morning, I peel ginger to add to smoothies (I like mine pretty spicy), and I also grate it with abandon into recipes like my Pomegranate-Ginger Short Ribs (page 171). Ginger has a boatload of antioxidants, so I feel like a health nut since I use it so much. It's great for everything from your skin to your overall health and preventing sickness. And while Black folk around these parts swear by ginger ale for tummy aches, I steep ginger in boiling water along with honey and (my fave) lemons.

7 cilantro

Cilantro is the most polarizing herb I can think of—some people love it, while others absolutely loathe it. It's my all-time favorite herb because it brings so much flavor to a dish, and it's thus a must for my Mexican- and Caribbean-inspired dishes, salsas, and so much more. Sometimes, I even add it to a pot of plain rice just to perk that baby up.

that I constantly reach for

1 smoked paprika

When you want to give a dish a seductive, smoky scent, nothing beats smoked paprika. It's especially fantastic in vegetarian and vegan dishes, such as Vegan Red Beans and Rice (page 141), where you may need to create more intense flavors.

2 cayenne

This punchy chile is indispensable when you want to add some heat to a dish. From starters to soups to my famous hot fried chicken (page 189), it's just not the same without the kick of cayenne, y'all.

3 cumin

I love how many different cuisines rely on cumin for its intense savory flavor, including Mexican, Indian, and Caribbean, just to name a few. I truly am at a loss when I start running low. If you want to really kick it up a notch, toast whole cumin seeds in a dry skillet over medium-low heat until aromatic, then grind them in your spice grinder for ground cumin that may convince you to never buy it pre-ground again.

4 diamond crystal kosher salt

I'm devoted to Diamond Crystal brand kosher salt in my kitchen. It's a pleasure to pinch with your fingers and has a texture that keeps you from overseasoning. I buy several boxes at a time and keep them in my pantry. The recipes in this book were developed with Diamond Crystal, so if you can't find it, use half of the indicated amount for fine sea salt and even less for table salt, and you should be all good.

5 garlic powder

For a while, using garlic powder was passé in the cool food crowd, but these days, it's making a comeback, y'all. It lends a milder garlic note to anything it touches, including spice rubs, soups, and stews.

6 onion powder

This is another one of my secret power-player ingredients. With a sweet, mild onion flavor that works wonders in dishes, onion powder is truly underappreciated and needs to get more love and recognition.

7 lawry's seasoned salt

Lawry's savory-sweet flavor profile is part of what makes my Cereal-Crusted Buffalo Chicken Tenders (page 61) and Crispy AF Air Fryer Green Tomatoes (page 55) so irresistible. They wouldn't be the same without this seasoned salt.

that I constantly reach for

1 ground allspice

Warm, zesty, spicy, and comforting, allspice is essential in my sweet arsenal when I want to impart a unique flavor profile to a baked good. The flavor is hard to describe, but I think it tastes like nutmeg, cloves, and cinnamon had a baby.

2 ground cinnamon

Speaking of cinnamon, it is a basic baking spice that most will have, and that's because it really adds a little something to anything and everything.

3 ground ginger

The mild kick and warming sensation that comes from ground ginger is unique and different from the flavor and heat of the fresh root. Ground ginger is a must in many baked desserts, such as my carrot cake (page 211), but is also incredible in savory dishes, like my sweet potato soup (page 99).

4 nutmeg

Keep whole nutmeg in your kitchen and grate it as needed. A good-quality rasp grater, such as a Microplane, serves double-duty as a nutmeg grater. Freshly grated nutmeg is incomparably fragrant, and you only need just a little bit since its flavor is so pronounced.

5 vanilla

I love using vanilla in my desserts, and a little goes a long way. I keep extract, paste (my fave), and whole beans on hand to add to sweet recipes. When searching for vanilla beans, which can get pricey, look for plump, moist-looking pods. And don't toss your scraped or used-up beans! Throw them in your sugar canister for fragrant vanilla sugar.

6 ground cloves

Intensity in spice form—that's what I consider cloves. I find cloves more potent than cinnamon, and I love to add them to baked goods year-round.

7 cardamom

Ginger's "baby cousin" (they're botanically related), fragrant, floral cardamom is a feisty spice that can warm a baked good like no other. It can be overpowering, which is why I add just a lil' bit, y'all, then sprinkle in more if need be.

1 solo time

People are often surprised to learn that I enjoy traveling by myself even though I have a family, but the introverted part of me craves solo trips. The part of me that's extroverted, of course, makes friends on the vacay, but I always turn down dinners and subsequent meetings, because I love dining by myself. Also, I love an amazing movie night alone. I've realized that if you can do these things alone, you truly love yourself.

2 a self-care ritual

I take an hour-long bath every night—I never miss one and nothing can stop me. I grab a good book; fill up the tub with hot water, Epsom salt, and bubbles; turn on my music; and soak until I turn into a raisin. This is essential, and my family knows not to bother me, knock on the door, or even utter a single word in the vicinity of the bathroom because I demand complete peace during this time. I turn on smooth

jazz (elevator music) or meditation music (the kind you hear at the spa) and just melt away.

3 dancing

There's a reason every Black function ends with a *Soul Train* line or group Cupid Shuffle experience. It's good for the soul. I dance anywhere and everywhere, even in the aisles at the grocery store. The funny thing is, no one looks at me like I'm crazy. They usually join in! You might catch me tap-dancing on my IG account, too. I've also been learning the choreography of old dance movies and epic music videos just for fun. Seriously, why not?

4 general silliness in everyday things

I love making up silly songs with insane lyrics and calling my brother to share them. I even have an ode to chicken nuggets—made with my boo Alesha (see page 61).

5 listening to Christmas music all year round

Don't tell me holiday music season is between Thanksgiving and December 26! In my heart, it's always Christmas, boos.

6 giving back

Any time I've served others or given back in any way, I've felt so much better about everything. When I was living in Chicago, I started a bake sale to raise money for anti-violence efforts. And I've taught baking at schools in the inner city.

7 field trips

During the COVID-19 pandemic, I had to find ways to entertain myself, and local field trips to places such as the zoo and water park really lifted my mood. Yes, adults can go to the zoo, theme parks, and all that jazz *alone*! I used to go to Disney World every year with my family *before* I had my baby girl, and it was so amazing to return to my youth in that way.

You can have the recipe for joy right in your fingertips, but you still gotta cook it, boos! —*jocelyn*

breakfast

Big Mama's hands told my family's stories: You could see the wisdom, love, courage, and strength in each coiled line and wrinkle. The hands that delicately sifted flour for cake batter, canned the fruit from her backyard trees, and masterfully cleaned greens also pulled me in for warm hugs and sculpted her buttery fluffed-to-the-heavens biscuits. When I was a young girl watching Big Mama make biscuits (which she did almost every single day for eighty years), much of my fascination resided in the strength of her hands and her ferocious spirit. She spent years perfecting the recipe she eventually passed on to me, improving her technique and making the biscuits lighter and fluffier with each batch. The life lesson I subconsciously learned was that success hinges on consistency—the most accomplished people I know are also the most consistent. They work until the job is done—and done right. I like to believe that I inherited this fighting spirit from Big Mama, and my twist on her biscuits with fig preserves is an homage to her.

cornmeal butter biscuits with big mama's fig preserves

MAKES 10 BISCUITS

FIG PRESERVES
12 ounces (340 grams) **fresh figs**, halved
1½ cups (300 grams) **granulated sugar**

BISCUITS
3¼ cups (406 grams) **all-purpose flour**, plus more as needed

½ cup (63 grams) **fine yellow cornmeal**
¼ cup (30 grams) **cornstarch**
2 tablespoons **granulated sugar**
4 teaspoons **baking powder**
1 tablespoon **kosher salt**
1 cup (2 sticks/226 grams) **unsalted butter**, cut into cubes and frozen for 20 minutes

1⅓ cups (316 grams) cold **whole milk**
1 large **egg**
1 tablespoon **unsalted butter**, melted, for brushing the biscuits
Flaky sea salt, such as fleur de sel or Maldon

CELEBRATE!
A new baking pan; honoring a family elder; that figs are in season; a potluck

recipe continues

1. **Make the preserves:** In a large heavy-bottomed pot, combine the figs and sugar with ¾ cup (168 grams) water. Bring the pot to a lively simmer over medium-low heat, then reduce the heat to low and gently simmer, stirring occasionally to prevent scorching on the bottom, until thickened, about 45 minutes. The syrup should coat the back of a spoon. Remove from the heat and let cool completely. Transfer to a 2-cup mason jar and let the preserves set up at room temperature, about 2 hours. Serve with biscuits, over ice cream, or generously slather on your morning toast. Since the preserves aren't put up using a hot water bath method, you can refrigerate them for up to 2 weeks.

2. **Make the biscuits:** In a large bowl, whisk together the flour, cornmeal, cornstarch, sugar, baking powder, and kosher salt until combined.

3. In the bowl with the flour mixture, using a pastry cutter or two butter knives, cut the cold butter into the flour mixture until it forms crumbs of varying sizes. This will take a bit of effort and arm strength, but I welcome a workout before buttery biscuit calories. Pour the milk into the butter-flour mixture and knead just until nearly all the flour is incorporated and forms a dough, about 2 minutes.

4. Lightly flour your work surface and turn the dough out onto it. Fold the dough over itself 4 times to develop a stiff dough.

5. Using a floured rolling pin, roll out the dough to a roughly 12 by 18-inch rectangle. Fold the dough into thirds, as if you were folding a letter. Then, fold the two short ends of the dough toward the center, wrap in plastic wrap, and refrigerate for 40 minutes.

6. Lightly reflour your work surface and rolling pin and remove the dough from the plastic wrap. Roll out the dough to a 1-inch-thick rectangle about 7 by 9 inches and cut crosswise into thirds. Stack the three rectangles on top of one other, then use your rolling pin to roll them together into another 1-inch-thick rectangle about 5 by 10 inches (the dimensions will alternate with each turn). Lightly reflour your work surface and rolling pin as needed while you work. Turn the rectangle a quarter turn, then repeat 3 more times, leaving the final long rectangle 1 to 1½ inches in height. Chillax in the fridge for 30 minutes.

7. Position a rack in the middle of the oven and preheat to 475°F. Line a large rimmed baking sheet with parchment paper.

8. Lightly flour your work surface and place the dough on top. Use a round cutter to cut round biscuits or a knife to cut the dough into about 10 squares and place them on the prepared baking sheet.

9. In a small bowl, whisk together the egg and 1 teaspoon water until combined. Brush the tops of the biscuits with the egg wash.

10. Bake for 10 minutes, then rotate the pan and bake for 5 to 7 minutes more, until the biscuits are golden brown and crisp on the outer edges. Brush immediately with the melted butter and sprinkle with the flaky salt. Serve warm, slathered with the fig preserves.

To me, the Bellini is the most special cocktail. I said what I said. When I turned twenty-one, I went to brunch with my parents to celebrate and ordered my first Bellini, which sounded special and sophisticated. The moment the drink arrived, I realized, *I'm all grown up. Here I am, sitting and having a drink with my 'rents.* Even now that I'm truly an adult, with a family, a mortgage, and a career (grown life with responsibilities hits different), a peach Bellini still feels magical, so this dressed-up coffee cake—made over with peach Bellini flavors—is *the* ultimate brunch menu item.

peach bellini brunch cake

MAKES ONE 12-CUP BUNDT CAKE (SERVES 12)

1 ripe medium **peach** (7 ounces)

BELLINI SIMPLE SYRUP
½ cup (112 grams) **dry sparkling wine**, such as champagne or prosecco, etc.
½ cup (100 grams) **granulated sugar**
¼ cup (65 grams) **fresh peach nectar**

CAKE
Nonstick baking spray
3 cups (375 grams) **all-purpose flour**
1 teaspoon **kosher salt**
1 teaspoon **baking powder**
½ teaspoon **baking soda**
1 cup plus 2 tablespoons (2¼ sticks/255 grams) **unsalted butter**, at room temperature
2 cups (400 grams) **granulated sugar**

3 large **eggs**, at room temperature
2 large **egg yolks**, at room temperature
1 teaspoon **vanilla extract**
¾ cup (168 grams) **dry sparkling wine**, such as champagne, prosecco, etc.

PEACH GLAZE
1½ cups (150 grams) sifted **confectioners' sugar**
3 tablespoons (50 grams) **fresh peach nectar**

1. Make the peach puree: Bring a small pot of water to a boil over high heat. Fill a medium bowl with water and ice (*ice ice, baby*—sorry, had to do that!). Using a sharp paring knife, gently score a large "x" on the non-stem end of the peach. Blanch the peach in the boiling water for about 2 minutes, then transfer it to the prepared ice bath and let cool, about 5 minutes. Once cool enough to handle, use your hands to slip off the skin, then halve and pit the peach. Transfer the flesh to a mini food processor, add 2 tablespoons water, and process until smooth. You should have about ¾ cup of peach puree. Set aside.

recipe continues

2. **Make the Bellini simple syrup:** In a small pot, combine the dry sparkling wine, granulated sugar, peach nectar, and 2 tablespoons of the peach puree, set over medium-high heat, and bring to a boil. Cook until the liquid has reduced by about a third (to about ¾ cup), 5 to 8 minutes. Remove from the heat and set aside to cool.

3. **Make the cake:** Position a rack in the middle of the oven and preheat to 350°F. Generously grease a 12-cup Bundt pan with the nonstick baking spray (see Note).

4. In a medium bowl, whisk together the flour, salt, baking powder, and baking soda until combined.

5. In the bowl of a stand mixer fitted with the whisk attachment (I love the whisk because it incorporates more air, boos!), beat the butter on medium-high speed until light and fluffy, about 2 minutes. Slowly add the granulated sugar and beat until very pale yellow and fluffy, about 5 minutes. Add the eggs one at a time, followed by the egg yolks and vanilla, beating well after each addition and scraping down the sides and bottom of the bowl as needed.

6. In a measuring cup with a spout, combine the dry sparkling wine and ¼ cup (60 grams) of the peach puree. Reduce the mixer speed to low and add the flour mixture in three additions, alternating with the champagne mixture, scraping the sides and bottom of the bowl as needed. Stop the mixer and give the batter a final stir by hand.

7. Pour the batter into the prepared pan and smooth the top. Bake for 55 minutes to 1 hour, rotating the pan midway through baking, until a toothpick inserted into the center of the cake comes out clean and the top of the cake is golden brown and starts to pull away from the sides of the pan. Transfer the pan to a wire rack and let cool for about 15 minutes. Turn the cake out onto the rack or a cake stand and let cool for another 20 minutes. Lightly cover the cake with aluminum foil or plastic wrap so it does not dry out.

8. **Assemble the cake:** Liberally poke the top of the cake with a skewer, then pour the Bellini simple syrup in batches over the entire cake, letting it seep in each time before adding more. It may seem like a ton of syrup, but don't stress it, boos—the cake is insanely delicious and moist when soaked through. Let the cake cool completely before glazing; otherwise, the glaze will slide right off the cake.

9. **Make the glaze:** In a small bowl, whisk together the confectioners' sugar and peach nectar until smooth and thick but still pourable. Drizzle the glaze over the cooled cake and let set for about 10 minutes. Serve with coffee or, you know, a Bellini, boos! Get at it!

note If you don't have nonstick baking spray, which has flour added to it for easy release, make a paste with 1 tablespoon flour, 1 tablespoon oil, and 1 tablespoon melted butter, and use a pastry brush to coat the inside of the pan with the paste.

CELEBRATE!
Mother's Day;
child's first words;
"I Want and Deserve
Cake" Day

Easy like Sunday morning is how I typically begin my days. They start with gratitude journaling, quiet time with daily affirmations playing in the background, a workout, then breakfast. Mornings are my time to create a blueprint for the day, and this frittata nourishes the body, mind, and spirit with eggs, andouille sausage, Cajun seasoning, and the holy trinity of onion, bell pepper, and celery. Plus, you don't have to babysit, flip, or give it much attention (looking at you, omelet), and it still slays.

jammin' frittata

SERVES 4 TO 6

1 tablespoon **vegetable oil** or other neutral oil
½ cup diced **sweet onion**
½ cup diced **green bell pepper**
¼ cup diced **celery**
1 teaspoon minced **fresh rosemary**
½ teaspoon **No-Salt Cajun Seasoning** (recipe follows) or store-bought

1 **andouille sausage**, sliced
½ cup shredded **cooked chicken breasts** or leftover rotisserie chicken
½ cup **cherry tomatoes**, halved
4 tablespoons (½ stick) **unsalted butter**, cut into pats
10 large **eggs**

Scant ¼ cup **heavy cream**
1 tablespoon **hot sauce**
Kosher salt and **freshly ground black pepper**
½ cup shredded **white cheddar cheese**
3 tablespoons chopped **fresh chives**

1. Position a rack in the middle of the oven and preheat to 400°F.

2. In an ovenproof 12-inch nonstick skillet, heat the oil over medium heat until shimmering. Add the onion, bell pepper, celery, rosemary, and Cajun seasoning, and cook, stirring occasionally, until tender, 6 to 7 minutes. Add the sausage and cook, stirring occasionally, until browned and warmed through, about 10 minutes.

3. Stir in the chicken, then spread the cherry tomatoes evenly over the mixture and top with pats of butter (hungry yet?). Reduce the heat to its lowest setting.

4. In a large bowl, whisk the eggs, cream, and hot sauce until combined. Lightly season with salt and pepper (remember, you got hot sauce and sausage adding heat and salt). Pour the mixture into the skillet and top with the cheese and chives. Cover and bake for 20 to 25 minutes, until the frittata is fluffy and golden around the edges.

5. Now let's do the wiggle, boos! Carefully, with mitted hands, hold the skillet and slightly jiggle the frittata. If the middle doesn't wiggle, it's all good, baby! Otherwise, return to the oven for another 2 to 3 minutes, then repeat the wiggle test.

6. Let the frittata cool in the pan for 5 to 10 minutes. Top with more salt and pepper, then slice and serve!

no-salt cajun seasoning

You can certainly buy Cajun seasoning at the store, but most of it comes with too much salt. Not to worry—I've got your no-salt solution right here, with a recipe that will allow you to control exactly how much (or little) salt you want in your dish, without sacrificing flavor. **MAKES ABOUT ⅓ CUP**

1 tablespoon **garlic powder**
2½ teaspoons **smoked paprika**
2 teaspoons **cayenne pepper**

2 teaspoons **freshly ground black pepper**
2 teaspoons **freshly ground white pepper**
2 teaspoons **dried oregano**
2 teaspoons **dried thyme**
1 teaspoon **onion powder**

In a small bowl, whisk together the garlic powder, paprika, cayenne, black pepper, white pepper, oregano, thyme, and onion powder until combined. Store in a lidded jar in a cool, dark place for up to 4 months.

CELEBRATE!
Birthday breakfast;
first morning of a
new job

This recipe is my love letter to myself. I love pancakes so much, I'd request them for my last meal, which would, obviously, be a twelve-course affair (don't make me choose just one!). My pancake love goes back to when I was little, and I would request a birthday breakfast at IHOP. Now that I'm grown up, I expect a lot of my pancakes: fluffy and light to absorb all that syrup, but with an incredible griddled exterior. And with this recipe, I give you both, boos!

the best classic pancakes

MAKES ABOUT 20 PANCAKES (SERVES 4 OR 5)

2 cups (266 grams) **cake flour**
⅓ cup (67 grams) **granulated sugar**
1 tablespoon **baking powder**
¾ teaspoon **kosher salt**
1⅓ cups (320 grams) **half-and-half**

1 cup (227 grams) **sour cream**
2 large **eggs**
2 tablespoons (28 grams) **unsalted butter**, melted and cooled, plus more for cooking and serving
1 teaspoon **vanilla extract**

Neutral oil, such as vegetable or canola, for cooking the pancakes
Maple syrup, for serving

1. Place a large rimmed baking sheet in the oven and preheat to 200°F.

2. In a large bowl, whisk together the flour, sugar, baking powder, and salt until combined.

3. In another large bowl, whisk together the half-and-half, sour cream, eggs, melted butter, and vanilla until combined. Gently stir the wet ingredients into the dry just until combined—the batter will have some lumps. Let sit for 10 to 15 minutes to hydrate—this will give you fluffier pancakes.

4. Heat a large cast-iron skillet over medium-low to medium heat until hot. Grease the surface with a small pat of butter and a small drizzle of oil. When the oil starts to shimmer and the butter foam subsides, add about ¼ cup of batter to the skillet. Cook until bubbles begin to form on top and the pancakes are golden brown on the bottom, 2 to 3 minutes, then gently flip and cook until golden on the bottom, 2 to 3 minutes. Resist the urge to flip the pancakes back and forth, as it will only toughen their texture. Transfer the cooked pancakes to the oven to keep warm and repeat with remaining batter, adding more butter and oil to your skillet as needed and adjusting the heat to prevent the pancakes from burning without cooking through. Serve warm, with the maple syrup and extra butter.

notes If you don't have cake flour on hand, weigh or measure out the same amount of all-purpose flour and take away 2 tablespoons flour per cup, then replace that flour with an equivalent amount of cornstarch and whisk thoroughly to combine.

I've always had a sunny, glass-half-full disposition that has people amazed, because they can't imagine me ever being angry or sad. The truth is that we all have days of rain in our lives. What has always helped me is that even on my worst days, I have faith that life will work out. And while I might not understand the full plan, I know that I can rise from anything.

For those tough moments, this popover recipe, with its sunny, citrusy notes and puffed "ascending above the storm" structure, puts me in a good mood. I love to watch them climb to great heights in the oven before slathering them with a honey-butter smear. That first bite is a reminder that "weeping may endure for a night, but joy cometh in the morning" (Psalms 30:5).

orange-lavender popovers

MAKES 12 POPOVERS

POPOVERS
4 large **eggs**, at room
   temperature
1½ cups lukewarm **whole milk**
1½ cups (188 grams) **all-purpose**
   flour
1½ tablespoons **lavender buds**
   (culinary grade)

1 tablespoon **granulated sugar**
1 teaspoon **kosher salt**
Finely grated **zest** of 2 large
   oranges
3 tablespoons (45 grams)
   unsalted butter, melted
Nonstick cooking spray

HONEY BUTTER
½ cup (1 stick/113 grams)
   unsalted butter, at room
   temperature
3 tablespoons **honey**
¼ teaspoon **kosher salt**, or more
   to taste

1. Make the popovers: Position a rack in the middle of the oven and preheat to 450°F. Place a 12-cup muffin tin or 6-cup popover pan in the oven to preheat. When the oven comes to temp, begin the batter.

2. In a large bowl (or 8-cup measuring cup), lightly beat the eggs to combine. Vigorously whisk the milk into the eggs until thoroughly incorporated and no streaks of egg yolk remain.

3. In a medium bowl, thoroughly whisk together the flour, lavender, sugar, and salt until aerated. You want to break up any clumps

and fluff up the dry ingredients. Sprinkle the dry ingredients over the egg mixture, add the zest, and whisk vigorously until tiny bubbles and froth develop. (We want this batter well mixed, y'all, so if you see large lumps, keep at it.) Quickly whisk in the melted butter just to combine.

4. Carefully remove the hot pan from the oven and spray it thoroughly with cooking spray. Quickly pour the batter into the prepared pan, filling each cup only about two-thirds to three-quarters full. Carefully place the pan back in your hot-as-hell oven. Bake for 15 minutes, then reduce the oven temperature to 375°F and bake for 15 to 20 minutes more, until the popovers turn a deep golden brown and are puffed to perfection. It's super important that you don't open the oven door while they're baking, as this could deflate them—if you need to see how the popovers are doing, turn on your oven light and keep an eye on them.

CELEBRATE!
The perfect breakfast before church service; a Zoom baking party

5. **Make the honey butter:** While the popovers are baking, in a medium bowl, whisk the butter until fluffy. Drizzle in the honey, add the salt, and mix until thoroughly incorporated. (Word of advice, consider making a double batch, because this butter is just fantastic to have for all occasions.)

6. Transfer the pan of popovers to a wire rack and run a butter knife around each popover to easily release them and get that steam out. Serve immediately with the honey butter because these babies deflate quickly.

I have a complicated relationship with cinnamon rolls. Ya see, I love each bite of their pillowy, gooey goodness, but I hate the long, tedious process of making them. As I get older, I realize more and more how precious time is, and my priorities have shifted from wanting to spend all day in the kitchen to wanting to spend it with my fam. Part of finding happiness is being in the moment and indulging a craving when it strikes. This cinnamon roll Dutch baby solves it all. The flavor of cinnamon rolls in mere minutes? Check! That irresistible cinnamon-sugar swirl? Check! The sweet, gooey icing that takes it over the top? Check, check, check!

blender cinnamon roll dutch baby

MAKES ONE 10-INCH PANCAKE (SERVES 2 TO 4)

CELEBRATE!
Birthday brunch;
Saturday morning
just cuz; a positive
pregnancy test

BATTER
3 tablespoons (42 grams) **unsalted butter**, divided
½ cup (128 grams) **half-and-half**, at room temperature
3 large **eggs**, at room temperature
1 teaspoon **vanilla extract**
½ cup (63 grams) **all-purpose flour**
1 tablespoon **granulated sugar**
¼ teaspoon **kosher salt**
¼ teaspoon **ground cinnamon**
⅛ teaspoon **freshly grated nutmeg**

SWIRL
4 tablespoons (½ stick/ 57 grams) **unsalted butter**, at room temperature
¼ cup packed (40 grams) **light brown sugar**
1½ teaspoons **ground cinnamon**
⅛ teaspoon **kosher salt**

GLAZE
2 tablespoons (30 grams) **cream cheese**, at room temperature
1 tablespoon (15 grams) **unsalted butter**, at room temperature
1 tablespoon **honey**
⅓ cup (40 grams) **confectioners' sugar**

1. Make the batter: Position a rack in the middle of the oven and preheat to 425°F.

2. In a small microwave-safe bowl, melt 2 tablespoons (30 grams) of the butter in the microwave (or melt the butter in a small saucepan over low heat). Set aside.

3. In a blender, combine the half-and-half, eggs, and vanilla. Blend on low for about 10 seconds, just to break up the eggs. Raise the speed to medium-low and add the melted butter in a thin, steady steam, just to incorporate. Stop the blender and add the flour, granulated sugar, salt, cinnamon, and nutmeg. Blend on high until smooth, about 1 minute, scraping the sides at least once midway through.

4. Let the batter hang out for 10 minutes to hydrate; it should be thin like pancake batter and will thicken slightly as it sits.

5. Make the swirl: While the batter thickens, in a medium bowl, stir together the softened butter, brown sugar, cinnamon, and salt until well combined. The mixture will have a gritty texture, but that's cool, boos. Transfer the mixture to a plastic zip-top bag, pressing it toward one corner, and set aside.

6. Bake the Dutch baby: Heat a 10-inch cast-iron skillet over high heat until hot. Melt the remaining 1 tablespoon butter until foamy. Swirl the butter around the bottom and up sides of the skillet to thoroughly coat, then pour the rested batter in the hot pan.

7. Cut off the tip of one corner of the plastic bag holding the swirl to make a small hole for easy piping (about ½ inch is fine). Starting in the center and working outward toward the edge of the pan, quickly pipe the swirl mixture on top in a spiral.

8. Transfer the skillet to the oven and bake for about 15 minutes, or until the Dutch baby is golden and gorgeously puffed. (The Dutch baby will deflate like an air mattress soon after being removed from the oven.)

9. Make the glaze: While the Dutch baby bakes, in a small bowl, whisk together the cream cheese, butter, and honey until thoroughly combined. Sift in the confectioners' sugar and whisk until smooth. (If you want to pipe the glaze, transfer it to a plastic zip-top bag with a tip snipped off or pastry bag fitted with a tip of your choosing, and pipe it in fun swirls or designs.)

10. Remove the Dutch baby from the oven and immediately pipe or spread the glaze over the top. Serve right away.

I may sound biased, but my mama's zucchini bread is the absolute best (sorry, banana bread). Here I share a fun twist on her delicious recipe because I'm a firm believer in infusing our lives with as much fun as possible (being a grown-up is serious enough as is). As a kid, I loved Cinnamon Toast Crunch for breakfast, and my brother and I would fill our bowls to the brim and go to town. So I decided to add this fun crunchy topping to the World's Greatest Zucchini Bread, and I dare you to make it and not grin from ear to ear while eating it!

cinnamon toast crunch zucchini bread

MAKES ONE 9 BY 5-INCH LOAF (SERVES 8)

CINNAMON TOAST CRUNCH TOPPING

2 tablespoons **Cinnamon Toast Crunch cereal**

2 tablespoons packed **light brown sugar**

1 tablespoon **all-purpose flour**

¾ teaspoon **ground cinnamon**

Pinch of **kosher salt**

1 tablespoon (15 grams) **unsalted butter**, melted

ZUCCHINI BREAD

Nonstick baking spray

1½ cups (188 grams) **all-purpose flour**

1¼ teaspoons **baking powder**

½ teaspoon **baking soda**

½ teaspoon **ground cinnamon**

½ teaspoon **kosher salt**

¼ teaspoon **freshly grated nutmeg**

2 large **eggs**, at room temperature

1 cup (200 grams) **granulated sugar**

½ cup (110 grams) **vegetable oil** or other neutral oil

1 teaspoon **vanilla extract**

2 cups (300 grams) coarsely grated **zucchini** (1 large or 2 medium), squeezed of excess liquid with your hands

1. **Make the topping:** In a small resealable bag, lightly crush the cereal into smaller pieces of varying sizes—you should have small crumbs and larger chunks in there. Transfer to a medium bowl, add the brown sugar, flour, cinnamon, and salt, and stir to combine. Drizzle in the butter and, using your hands or a fork, mix until the topping looks like wet sand, then set aside.

2. **Make the zucchini bread:** Position a rack in the middle of the oven and preheat to 350°F.

Grease an 8 by 4½ by 2¾-inch loaf pan with nonstick baking spray and line it with a piece of parchment paper, leaving at least a 2-inch overhang on both longer sides.

3. In a medium bowl, whisk together the flour, baking powder, baking soda, cinnamon, salt, and nutmeg until combined.

4. In a large bowl and using a handheld mixer, beat the eggs on high speed until frothy, about 1 minute. Add the granulated sugar and beat on high to incorporate, about 1 minute.

5. With the mixer running on medium-high speed, add the oil in a steady stream and beat until the mixture has the thickness and texture of mayonnaise, about 1 minute. Add the vanilla and beat until incorporated, about 15 seconds. Add the dry ingredients to the wet ingredients and mix on low speed just to combine. Using a rubber spatula, fold in the zucchini just until combined—the batter will be very thick.

6. Transfer the batter to the prepared loaf pan and smooth the top. Evenly sprinkle the topping over it.

7. Bake for 1 hour to 1 hour 15 minutes, until a toothpick or cake tester inserted into the center comes out clean and the loaf starts to pull away from the sides of the pan. Let cool in the pan on a wire rack for 15 minutes, then use the overhanging parchment to lift the bread from the pan and set it on the rack. Let cool completely, ideally overnight, before slicing and serving (letting it rest really helps set the bread's texture).

CELEBRATE!
First day of school; rainy day bake; kid baking project day

To my ambitious, everyday-you're-hustling, not-just-chasing-but-living-dreams, know-your-complete-worth-and-won't-settle-for-less, don't-quit-till-you-get-it-ALL boos, I see you, queens! When you get it cracking at five a.m., spoil yourself with a lil' "dessert" for breakfast that still packs a nourishing punch. Here you get all the banana pudding feels in a healthier package. Frozen bananas give that sensational creamy texture when blended with yogurt, then we go HAM on the toppings! Go off with a little hemp seed, flaked coconut, and glorious fresh fruit. Add your favorite granola, too. I threw in a few Nilla wafers for authenticity's sake. Go out and own it!

banana pudding smoothie bowl

SERVES 2

CELEBRATE!
The morning before a big meeting or presentation; a nice reward after a challenging workout

4 peeled, sliced, and **frozen bananas**
1 cup **unsweetened coconut milk Greek yogurt**
½ cup **oat**, **almond**, or **coconut milk** (my preference is oat milk)
1 teaspoon **vanilla extract**

2 teaspoons **maple syrup**
¼ teaspoon **ground cinnamon**
¼ teaspoon **ground ginger**
½ cup your fave **granola**
6 **vanilla-flavored wafer cookies**, such as Nilla wafers
¼ cup **unsweetened flaked coconut**

1 **ripe banana**, peeled and sliced
1 tablespoon **hemp seeds**
1 **mango**, peeled, pitted, and diced
Handful of **fresh raspberries**

1. Place the frozen bananas in a heavy-duty blender (I like to let them chill in there for 3 to 5 minutes, which softens them up a bit so they blend better). Add the yogurt, milk, vanilla, maple syrup, cinnamon, and ginger and blend until smooth, starting on low speed and gradually increasing to high, 1 to 2 minutes. Pause that blender and use a flexible spatula to scrape down the sides, then briefly blend again, starting on low speed and gradually increasing to high, to make sure everything gets incorporated.

2. Divide the smoothie between two shallow bowls. Top with the granola, cookies, coconut, banana, hemp seeds, mango, and raspberries and dig in.

The bones of this recipe come from my amazing aunt Beverly, my daddy's baby sis. She is a mean baker with a heart of gold and a sweet-as-pie disposition and a total boss in the kitchen. Ever since I was little, I loved visits to St. Louis to see her, my uncle Richard, and my cousins Raquel and Keisha. We'd spend most of the time laughing so hard we couldn't breathe and staying up late to watch movies. Aunt Bev's banana bread, made perfectly moist by sour cream, is particularly special, and it inspired this recipe, a spin on Elvis's favorite peanut-butter-banana-bacon sandwich. It seemed pretty genius to me when I thought of it. Boss moves!

the elvis banana bread

MAKES ONE 9 BY 5-INCH LOAF (SERVES 8)

CELEBRATE!
Your first sip of coffee; welcoming new neighbors; care package for a friend

3 slices **bacon**
Nonstick baking spray
1 cup (200 grams) **granulated sugar**
½ cup (1 stick/113 grams) **unsalted butter**, melted
2 large **eggs**, at room temperature

2 very **ripe medium bananas**, peeled and mashed
½ cup (113 grams) **sour cream**, at room temperature
2 teaspoons **vanilla extract**
1½ cups (188 grams) **all-purpose flour**

1½ teaspoons **baking powder**
½ teaspoon **baking soda**
½ teaspoon **kosher salt**
1¼ cups (220 grams) **peanut butter chips**, divided (see Note)

1. Position a rack in the middle of the oven and preheat to 450°F. Set a wire rack on a rimmed 13 by 18-inch baking sheet.

2. Place the bacon on the rack and roast until crisped up, about 20 minutes. (If you want, save the bacon drippings for frying eggs, roasting vegetables, or even adding to collard greens, my mama's trick.) Remove from the oven and reduce to 350°F. Let the bacon cool to the touch, then break it up or chop it into small pieces.

3. Spray a 9 by 5-inch loaf pan with nonstick baking spray and line it with a piece of parchment paper, leaving at least a 2-inch overhang on both longer sides.

4. In the bowl of a stand mixer fitted with the paddle attachment or in a large bowl and using a handheld mixer, beat the sugar and melted butter on medium speed until combined. Add the eggs one at a time and beat on medium-high speed until incorporated and the mixture is glossy and luxurious, about 2 minutes. Add the bananas and beat on medium speed to combine, followed by the sour cream. Add the vanilla and beat until incorporated.

5. In a medium bowl, whisk together the flour, baking powder, baking soda, and salt until combined. Add the dry ingredients to the wet ingredients and stir with a flexible spatula to combine. Fold in 1 cup (175 grams) of the peanut butter chips.

6. Transfer the batter to the prepared loaf pan and smooth the top. Sprinkle with the chopped bacon bits and the remaining ¼ cup (45 grams) peanut butter chips. Bake for 55 to 65 minutes, until a skewer inserted into the center comes out pretty darn clean. Transfer the pan to a wire rack and let cool completely. Run a butter knife around the perimeter of the pan, then use the overhanging parchment to lift the bread out of the pan. Slice and serve.

note Sometimes even the most well-stocked stores lack the very thing we need in these streets. But don't despair, boos! If you can't find peanut butter chips, just use chocolate instead. Or use half peanut butter chips and half chocolate chips for the best of both worlds. Even if it doesn't totally mimic Elvis's famed favorite sandwich, I'm sure the King wouldn't object to a little creativity, especially where chocolate is involved!

Surround yourself with good food and good vibes only! —*jocelyn*

appetizers & snacks

During my college heyday, my roommates and I would throw mean parties in our apartment. They would get so turnt up, I wouldn't recognize half the guests midway through the night. This recipe is inspired by our party days, where we scraped together the most economical and barest of ingredients and transformed them into impeccable hors d'oeuvres. In this pretzel monkey bread, each doughy, salty piece is made from refrigerated biscuit dough that you won't believe wasn't a pretzel to begin with! The key is to buy the buttermilk variety and not the flaky kind (I repeat: NOT the flaky kind). And the cheese dip? Baby, bye! *PHOTOGRAPH ON PAGE 50*

easy pretzel monkey bread with beer-cheese dip

SERVES 8 TO 10

MONKEY BREAD
Nonstick baking spray
⅓ cup (60 grams) **baking soda**
2 (16-ounce/454-gram) tubes refrigerated **buttermilk biscuit dough**, such as Pillsbury (see headnote)
4 tablespoons (½ stick/ 57 grams) **unsalted butter**
Flaky sea salt, such as Maldon or fleur de sel, for sprinkling

BEER-CHEESE DIP
2 tablespoons (30 grams) **unsalted butter**
2 tablespoons **all-purpose flour**
1⅓ cups (336 grams) **dark beer** (you can drink what's left in the can)
8 ounces (225 grams) **sharp cheddar cheese**, coarsely shredded (see Note)

8 ounces (225 grams) **Monterey Jack cheese**, coarsely shredded (see Note)
1 teaspoon **chili powder**
1 teaspoon **garlic powder**
½ teaspoon **smoked paprika**
Kosher salt and **freshly ground black pepper**

1. Make the monkey bread: Position a rack in the middle of the oven and preheat to 350°F. Generously grease the inside of a 10-inch Bundt pan with nonstick baking spray. Line a large rimmed baking sheet with paper towels or a clean kitchen towel.

2. Fill a medium pot with 5 cups water, add the baking soda, and bring to a boil over high heat.

3. Remove the dough from the tubes, cut each biscuit in half, and roll each piece into a ball—you should have 32 balls. When the water comes to a boil, add the dough balls to the water, working in batches to avoid overcrowding, and cook until the dough puffs up slightly and floats to the very top of the water, 15 to 30 seconds. Using a spider or slotted spoon, transfer the dough balls to the prepared baking sheet to drain. Repeat with the remaining dough balls.

CELEBRATE!
Low-key karaoke
with the homies;
half-birthday
celebration

4. In a glass measuring cup, melt the butter in the microwave. Arrange the dough balls in a single layer in the prepared Bundt pan and brush generously with the melted butter, then sprinkle with the flaky salt. Repeat with the remaining dough, butter, and salt. Bake for about 30 minutes, until the dough turns a beautiful golden brown. Cover the top of the pan with a piece of aluminum foil and bake for about 15 minutes more, until the internal temperature of the monkey bread reaches 200°F. Remove the foil and bake for 5 minutes more, or until richly burnished.

5. Make the beer-cheese dip: In a medium pot, melt the butter over medium heat. Whisk in the flour and keep whisking until it turns pale buttercup yellow, 1 to 2 minutes. Slowly whisk in the beer until the mixture is smooth and no lumps remain, then cook, whisking, until the liquid thickens, bubbles, and turns the color of light gravy, 5 to 6 minutes. Turn off the heat, then stir in both cheeses and whisk until completely smooth and creamy. Whisk in the chili powder, garlic powder, and paprika and season with salt and pepper. Transfer to a small serving bowl.

6. Remove the monkey bread from the oven and let cool in the pan for 5 minutes. Run a butter knife or offset spatula around the edges of the pan, then turn the monkey bread out onto a large platter. Serve warm, with beer-cheese dip on the side.

note Here you want to shred the cheese yourselves, boos, because preshredded cheese has added anticaking agents, which may result in your sauce not becoming smooth and uniform.

My daddy's grandmother Louvenia used to grow a garden full of green tomatoes. She'd pick them while they were still green, then blanch them, peel them, and put them up, tuck them into sandwiches, and whir them into soups. And, of course, she'd dredge them in cornmeal and fry them in her cast-iron skillet like a boss. So when my daddy started growing his own tomatoes, I realized what a special culinary treasure they are (plus, I grew up watching the eponymous movie!).

Since green tomatoes have such a brief season, I like to celebrate them as much as I can and fry them while the getting's good. To me, they are a reminder to treasure those quickly passing moments in life and truly make the most of every second.

crispy AF air fryer green tomatoes

SERVES 4

CELEBRATE!
Learning a new hobby; back-to-school dinner; celebrating that it's finally (!) tomato season

GREEN TOMATOES
6 tablespoons **plain bread crumbs**
½ cup plus 2 tablespoons **all-purpose flour**, divided
2 tablespoons **yellow cornmeal**
1 teaspoon **seasoned salt**, such as Lawry's
½ teaspoon **smoked paprika**
¼ teaspoon **cayenne pepper**
½ teaspoon **lemon pepper** or ¼ teaspoon freshly ground black pepper and ¼ teaspoon finely grated lemon zest
½ teaspoon **garlic powder**
½ teaspoon **onion powder**
⅛ teaspoon **mustard powder**
2 large **eggs**
2 teaspoons **hot sauce**
2 **green tomatoes** (about 1 pound 10 ounces total), sliced ¼ inch thick (ends reserved; see Note) and thoroughly dried with paper towels
Kosher salt and **freshly ground black pepper**
Nonstick cooking spray
2 tablespoons chopped **fresh flat-leaf parsley**, for serving
Lemon wedges, for serving

REMOULADE
½ cup **mayonnaise**
1 tablespoon **dill pickle relish** or 1 tablespoon or so of caper brine
1½ teaspoons **fresh lemon juice**
1½ teaspoons **hot sauce**
1 teaspoon **capers**, drained and coarsely chopped
Generous ½ teaspoon **smoked paprika**
½ teaspoon **Creole mustard** or yellow mustard
½ teaspoon **Worcestershire sauce**
¼ teaspoon **onion powder**
1 **garlic clove**, minced or finely grated

recipe continues

1. Line a large rimmed baking sheet with parchment paper.

2. **Prepare the tomatoes:** In a brown paper bag, large zip-top bag, or shallow bowl, combine the bread crumbs, 2 tablespoons of the flour, the cornmeal, seasoned salt, paprika, cayenne, lemon pepper, garlic powder, onion powder, and mustard powder and shake until well combined. Transfer the mixture to a shallow plate. Put the remaining ½ cup flour in a separate shallow bowl.

3. In a deep pie dish or large shallow bowl, whisk together the eggs and hot sauce and set aside.

4. Sprinkle the tomato slices with salt and black pepper on both sides. Using a fork and working with one tomato slice at a time, dip it in the all-purpose flour, followed by the egg mixture, letting the excess drip back into the bowl. Finally, dip the coated tomato slice into the seasoned bread crumbs and transfer to the prepared baking sheet. (Using a fork for the coating process will ensure a neater result, as fingers and/or tongs tend to rub off the breading, and we want to keep all that flavor, boos.) Repeat with the remaining tomato slices. Let the slices sit for about 10 minutes—this allows the coating to really adhere.

5. **Make the remoulade:** In a medium bowl, whisk together the mayonnaise, relish, lemon juice, hot sauce, capers, paprika, mustard, Worcestershire, onion powder, and garlic until smooth. Cover and refrigerate until ready to serve.

6. **Air-fry the tomatoes:** Set an air fryer to 400°F. Lightly spray the basket of the air fryer with cooking spray. Working in batches to avoid overcrowding, add the tomato slices to the basket and liberally spray the top of each slice with cooking spray to coat. Air-fry for 5 to 6 minutes, then remove the basket, gently flip the tomatoes, and spray with cooking spray. Air-fry for another 5 to 6 minutes, depending on the thickness of slices, until golden brown on the outside but still juicy and tender on the inside. Transfer the tomatoes to a wire rack and let cool for 5 minutes. Repeat with the remaining tomato slices.

7. When ready to serve, transfer the tomatoes to a serving plate, garnish with the parsley, and serve with the remoulade and lemon wedges on the side.

note I like to save my green tomato ends for salads—they add a delightfully tangy note. My daddy, on the other hand, likes to quick-pickle them. In a jar big enough to hold the tomato ends, combine apple cider vinegar or white wine vinegar, a little water, black pepper, salt, and brown sugar and swirl the jar to dissolve the salt. Add the tomato ends, screw on the lid, and refrigerate overnight. The next day, you'll have lightly pickled tomato slices to add to sandwiches or burgers.

I remember when I decided to truly take the plunge and start a food blog. Few were doing it for fun, and even fewer were making an actual living from it. Someone once told me, "You discover who you are when you take a path less traveled." The decision to make a career out of sharing my family's legacy recipes, as well as recipes I've leveled up, didn't have a road map and has been more difficult than people might think. It requires many skills, from photography to styling to recipe development, which just happened to be one of my favorite parts.

Take these meatballs, for example: They are the quintessential Black folks' party app, and my family always served them for festive gatherings, like my prom send-off and college trunk party. They're typically made with ground beef—here I give them a remix with lamb, but all in all, I stay true to what made them special in the first place: that unbelievable sticky-sweet spiced sauce. I hope that when someone makes this recipe for the first time, it'll fit right into their life, like a well-made glove. It's moments like these, being invited into someone's space when they make one of my recipes, that have made me truly grateful for all the blessings that food blogging has provided me.

bbq lamb meatballs

MAKES 16 MEATBALLS (SERVES 4 TO 8)

MEATBALLS

1 pound **ground lamb**

¼ cup **plain bread crumbs**

3 tablespoons **Mesquite Seasoning**, recipe follows

1 tablespoon **Worcestershire sauce**

1 tablespoon **mayonnaise**

1 large **egg**, beaten

2 **garlic cloves**, minced or finely grated

BARBECUE SAUCE

1½ teaspoons **extra-virgin olive oil**

½ small **yellow onion**, finely diced

1 **garlic clove**, minced or finely grated

½ (24-ounce) bottle **ketchup** (1¼ cups)

½ cup **crushed pineapple** with juices

¼ cup packed **dark brown sugar**

1½ tablespoons **maple syrup**

1 tablespoon **apple cider vinegar**

1½ teaspoons **Dijon mustard**

1½ teaspoons **Worcestershire sauce**

1 teaspoon **hickory liquid smoke**

1 teaspoon **Mesquite Seasoning**, recipe follows

½ teaspoon **kosher salt**

CELEBRATE!
Housewarming; baby shower; college trunk party

recipe continues

1. Make the meatballs: Position a rack in the middle of the oven and preheat to 375°F. Line a large rimmed baking sheet with parchment paper.

2. Now it's time to get those hands dirty, homies. Set a bowl of water near your workspace (trust this). In a medium bowl and using your hands, mix the lamb, bread crumbs, mesquite seasoning, Worcestershire, mayonnaise, egg, and garlic until well combined. Using a spoon, shape the mixture into golf ball–size meatballs and transfer them to the prepared baking sheet. Dampen your hands with water between forming meatballs to prevent the mixture from sticking to your palms.

3. Bake for 15 to 18 minutes, until fully cooked through and evenly browned. Remove from the oven and set aside.

4. Make the barbecue sauce: In a large saucepan, heat the olive oil over medium heat until shimmering. Add the onion and cook, stirring, until softened, 3 to 4 minutes. Add the garlic and cook, stirring, until aromatic, about 15 seconds. Stir in the ketchup, pineapple, brown sugar, maple syrup, vinegar, mustard, Worcestershire, liquid smoke, mesquite seasoning, and salt until fully incorporated. Bring to a boil, then reduce the heat to medium-low and cook, stirring occasionally, until the sauce has thickened, about 15 minutes. Remove from the heat.

5. Add the cooked meatballs to the sauce and gently stir until the meatballs are coated. Cook until the meatballs are warmed through, about 5 minutes more, then remove from the heat. Serve hot.

mesquite seasoning

This versatile seasoning is useful in several recipes, and you can apply it to different cuts of meat, pork loin, turkey burgers, and/ or salmon fillets.

MAKES ABOUT ¾ CUP

2½ tablespoons packed **dark brown sugar**
1 tablespoon **kosher salt**
1 tablespoon **smoked paprika**
1 tablespoon **chipotle chile powder**
2 teaspoons **garlic powder**
2 teaspoons **onion powder**
2 teaspoons **freshly ground black pepper**
2 teaspoons **ground cumin**
2 teaspoons **dried thyme**
1½ teaspoons **cayenne pepper**

In a medium bowl, whisk together the brown sugar, salt, paprika, chile powder, garlic powder, onion powder, black pepper, cumin, thyme, and cayenne until combined. Store in lidded jar in a cool, dark place for up to 3 months.

CELEBRATE!
Chill-mode date night; game days (we play Taboo on ours!)

These chicken tenders are dedicated to my singing homie Alesha, with whom I went to Clark Atlanta University, a famed HBCU in Georgia. Alesha and I were super-studious, top of all our classes, but when we weren't reviewing our notes, we'd walk up and down the strips at the colleges, such as Morehouse and Spelman, and sing made-up songs. Students would stop and gather to hear them, and one of our hits was a bop called "McNugget Yeah," an ode to chicken nuggets, strips, fingers, and, of course, tenders. These genius Buffalo chicken tenders are inspired by our hit song, and adding a sweet cereal to the coating makes them sweet, salty, and insanely crunchy. It's probably the unexpected crushed Cap'n Crunch cereal that takes these to another level (bet you didn't see that comin').

cereal-crusted buffalo chicken tenders

SERVES 4 TO 6

1½ pounds **chicken breast tenderloins**
2 cups well-shaken **buttermilk**
1½ cups finely crushed **Cap'n Crunch cereal**
1 cup **all-purpose flour**

3 tablespoons **seasoned salt**, such as Lawry's (see Note)
2 teaspoons **sweet paprika**
2 teaspoons **freshly ground black pepper**
½ teaspoon **garlic powder**
2 teaspoons **whole milk**

6 cups **canola oil**, for frying
⅓ cup **hot sauce**, such as Frank's RedHot Wings (it's bomb on these!)
4 tablespoons (½ stick) **salted butter**

1. In a large bowl, submerge the chicken in the buttermilk, cover, and refrigerate for at least 2 hours or up to 8 hours.

2. When ready to fry, in a medium bowl, whisk together the cereal, flour, seasoned salt, paprika, pepper, and garlic powder until combined. Drizzle in the milk and stir well.

3. Using tongs, lift the chicken tenders out of the buttermilk, letting the excess drip back into the bowl, then dip them in the seasoned flour, thoroughly coating each piece and using your free hand to scoop and press the coating onto the chicken to help it adhere. Transfer to a large rimmed baking sheet and repeat with the remaining chicken. Let sit until the coating has set, 10 to 15 minutes—this helps the coating adhere and stay on during the frying.

recipe continues

4. Position a rack in the middle of the oven and preheat to 275°F.

5. Set a wire rack on a large rimmed baking sheet and keep it near your work area. Fill a heavy-bottomed medium pot, Dutch oven, or deep-fryer with oil to a depth of 2½ to 3 inches and heat over medium-high heat. This is my test for checking when the oil is ready: Big Mama always tossed a tiny bit of flour into the oil, and if it began to fry and sizzle, the oil was ready. Or test the heat with a wooden spoon: Stick the bottom of the spoon into the oil; if ample bubbles surround it, the oil's ready to go, boos.

6. Working in batches to avoid overcrowding, fry the chicken tenders until golden brown, 2 to 3 minutes per side, depending on thickness. Transfer to the wire rack and let drain for 1 minute.

7. While the first batch of chicken is frying, in a small saucepan, combine the hot sauce and butter and warm over low heat until the butter has melted, about 3 minutes. Whisk the sauce to combine and remove from the heat.

8. When you've fried all the tenders, transfer them to a large bowl and toss with half the sauce until completely coated. If, like me, you prefer your wings really saucy, add the rest of the sauce, toss, and serve immediately.

note Seasoned salt varies from maker to maker, so keep that in mind when seasoning. I like Lawry's brand, but you may have something else more easily available. Remember the rule of seasoning: You can always add more, but you can't take it away, so start with less, just to be safe, and add more to taste as needed.

The Black community has a thing for Flamin' Hots, fo' sho'—Doritos, Cheetos, you name it. You always have a bag of these at school, after school—this is what we do. Separately, I don't know anybody who doesn't love mozzarella cheese sticks. It's cheese, it's in stick form, and there's the magic cheese pull. The traditional way of making mozzarella sticks is cool, but I wanted to see what would happen if I combined one of my all-time favorite snacks with another.

If you don't want to make marinara sauce, as Ina and my boo Sunny Anderson say, "Store-bought is fine." Rao's is pretty bomb and a great sub, but honestly, if you have the time, this homemade sauce is bangin'!

flamin' hot doritos fried mozzarella cheese sticks

SERVES 4 TO 6

CELEBRATE! Monopoly night; solo weekend; girls' night

MOZZARELLA STICKS
2 cups (2 ounces) crumbled **Doritos**, preferably Flamin' Hot flavor (see Note)
1 cup **all-purpose flour**
2 tablespoons **Italian Seasoning** (recipe follows) or store-bought
4 teaspoons **garlic powder**
4 teaspoons **onion powder**
4 teaspoons **kosher salt**

2 teaspoons **freshly ground black pepper**
2 large **eggs**, lightly beaten
12 **mozzarella sticks**, whole-milk or part-skim
Nonstick cooking spray

MARINARA
2 tablespoons **extra-virgin olive oil**
4 **garlic cloves**, smashed and peeled

1 (28-ounce) can **whole tomatoes**, preferably San Marzano
2 teaspoons **Italian Seasoning** (recipe follows) or store-bought
1 teaspoon **kosher salt**, plus more if needed
1 teaspoon **granulated sugar**
1 **bay leaf**
8 **fresh basil leaves**

1. Prepare the mozzarella sticks: Line a large rimmed baking sheet with waxed paper. In a food processor, pulse the Doritos until they are the texture of bread crumbs. Transfer to a medium bowl, then add the flour, Italian seasoning, garlic powder, onion powder, salt, and pepper and whisk until combined.

recipe continues

2. In a small bowl, whisk together the eggs and 2 tablespoons water until combined.

3. Dip a mozzarella stick in the Dorito crumb mixture just to dust it, then dip it in the egg and let the excess drip off. Return it to the Dorito crumb mixture and, using a small spoon, cover the cheese stick in the mixture, then use your fingers to gently but firmly roll it in the crumb mixture to coat. You want a generous coating that adheres to the cheese. Transfer to the prepared baking sheet and repeat with the remaining cheese sticks. Transfer the cheese sticks to the freezer for 30 minutes to 1 hour; do not discard the crumb mixture or egg.

4. Remove the cheese sticks from the freezer and repeat the breading sequence, building a generous second coating that adheres to the first. Return the cheese sticks to the freezer for 30 minutes to 1 hour.

5. Make the marinara: In a small saucepan, heat the olive oil over medium heat until shimmering. Add the garlic and cook, stirring, until golden brown, 2 to 4 minutes.

6. Pour the tomatoes into a large bowl and squeeze them with your hands to break them up into small bits (let's get dirty in the kitchen, boos). Add the tomatoes to the saucepan, followed by the Italian seasoning, salt, sugar, and bay leaf. Bring the mixture to a simmer, then reduce the heat to medium-low and cook, stirring occasionally, until the sauce thickens, about 20 minutes. Taste and season with additional salt, if desired. Remove from the heat and let cool for about 5 minutes. Discard the bay leaf, then transfer the sauce to a blender, add the basil, and blend until smooth. Transfer to a bowl and keep warm.

7. Air-fry the mozzarella sticks: Preheat an air fryer to 390°F. Lightly spray the air fryer basket with cooking spray.

8. Working in batches to avoid overcrowding, place the cheese sticks in the basket and generously spray them with cooking spray. Air-fry for 6 minutes, rotating the sticks halfway through, until golden brown and just barely starting to ooze cheese. Transfer to a plate and repeat with the remaining cheese sticks. Let cool for a few minutes before serving with marinara.

note If you can't find the Flamin' Hot flavor, add cayenne to the flour mixture when you add the Doritos.

italian seasoning

Have I mentioned yet that making your own seasoning mix sets you up nicely with easy and inexpensive edible gifts? They are perfect for housewarmings, holidays, and any time you want to make someone's day. As with the other spice mixes in this chapter, customize yours to highlight your favorite spices and herbs, or add a surprising twist. MAKES A SCANT ⅓ CUP

1 tablespoon **dried basil**
1 tablespoon **dried oregano**
1 tablespoon **dried rosemary**
1 tablespoon **dried thyme**
1½ teaspoons **garlic powder**
1½ teaspoons **crushed red pepper flakes**

In a small bowl, whisk together the basil, oregano, rosemary, thyme, garlic powder, and red pepper flakes until combined. Store in a lidded jar in a cool, dark place for up to 4 months.

When it comes to celebrating, nothing makes me more excited than awards season. From the Screen Actors Guild Awards to the Oscars, the love is so real. I majored in mass media arts with a minor in film—a fun fact many don't know about me—and I've always wanted to be a film director. And when I met my husband, Fred, I realized he has this insane passion for movies like I do. We'd go to independent movie screenings and be two of six people total in the theater, and we loved it. To this day, we come up with Academy Awards predictions and then keep track of who gets more of them right.

After our daughter, Harmony, came along, we wanted to re-create the magic of going to the movies, but in the comfort of our living room. It's hard to beat this popcorn, a good movie, and the chill vibes of home.

maple–brown butter pancetta popcorn

MAKES ABOUT 8 CUPS (SERVES 4 TO 8)

CELEBRATE!
Netflix-and-chill night; Oscars (or other movie awards) night; sorority meetup

8 slices **pancetta** or bacon (4½ ounces) or 1 (4-ounce) package chopped pancetta
½ cup (1 stick) **salted butter**

⅓ cup **maple syrup**
½ teaspoon **kosher salt**, plus more to taste

8 cups **popped popcorn** (from about ⅓ cup unpopped kernels)

1. Position a rack in the middle of the oven and preheat to 450°F. Set a wire rack over a large rimmed baking sheet.

2. Place the pancetta slices on the rack and bake for 15 to 20 minutes, until the pancetta is crispy and golden brown. Let the pancetta cool completely on the rack, then finely chop it and set aside; reserve the drippings on the baking sheet.

3. In a medium saucepan, melt the butter over medium heat, then cook until the solids brown and the butter smells nutty, about 6 minutes. Reduce the heat to low and whisk in the maple syrup, half the drippings, half the pancetta, and the salt until combined. (Reserve the rest of the pancetta fat for another use.)

4. In a large bowl, pour the butter syrup over the popcorn and gently mix to evenly coat. Top with the remaining pancetta and serve.

For Black folks, eating lemon pepper wings is almost a religious experience, all blessed vibez, with each bite resulting in a "thank you, God" shout and mini praise dance. They're essential at football games, card nights, and chill-mode nights at the crib. Zesty, citrusy, and pucker-worthy, this version is vegan *and* gluten-free because I want everyone to experience the magic. I use meaty oyster mushrooms that, when fried, give real chicken a run for its money. The double-dredge technique creates such a crisp exterior that you truly hear that crunch—the mark of a true fried wing. They're then tossed in what I call "liquid gold": a rich, buttery, lemony glaze, with a hint of sweet stickiness. Seriously, ain't no thing but a chicken wing.

agave–lemon pepper wingz

SERVES 4 TO 6

CELEBRATE!
Football season; a homie game of spades; a cozy, chill night in

WINGZ
2½ cups **rice flour**
1½ tablespoons **seasoned salt**, such as Lawry's
¼ cup **cornstarch**
2 teaspoons **lemon pepper**
1 teaspoon **freshly ground black pepper**
1 teaspoon **sweet paprika**
1 teaspoon **garlic powder**
½ teaspoon **cayenne pepper**

2 cups **oat milk** or other plant-based milk
2 tablespoons **apple cider vinegar**
1 tablespoon **hot sauce**, such as Tabasco
4 cups **vegetable oil** or other neutral oil, for frying
1 pound **oyster mushrooms**

LEMON PEPPER GLAZE
¼ cup **vegan butter**, melted

¼ cup **agave syrup**
2 teaspoons **fresh lemon juice**
¾ teaspoon **lemon pepper**, plus more as needed
Pinch of **freshly ground black pepper**

Chopped **fresh flat-leaf parsley**, for serving
Lemon wedges, for serving

1. **Make the wingz:** Set a wire rack over a large rimmed baking sheet. In a large plastic storage bag or paper bag, combine the flour, seasoned salt, cornstarch, lemon pepper, black pepper, paprika, garlic powder, and cayenne and shake to mix thoroughly. Slide to the side.

2. In a medium bowl, whisk together the oat milk, vinegar, and hot sauce until combined.

3. In a small heavy-bottomed pot, heat the oil until it registers 350°F on an instant-read thermometer.

4. Working with one mushroom at a time, use your hands or tongs to dip each mushroom in the milk mixture, letting the excess drip back into the bowl, then dredge it in the flour mixture. Repeat the dredging process again, placing the mushrooms on the wire rack as you go.

5. If you don't have an instant-read thermometer and want to make sure the oil is ready, drop a small piece of the mushroom in—it should immediately start to vigorously bubble. Set another wire rack over another large rimmed baking sheet or line the pan with paper towels or clean kitchen towels. Working in batches to avoid overcrowding, use tongs to gently place a few mushrooms in the hot oil. Fry the shrooms, turning them and adjusting the heat as needed, until they're golden brown deliciousness, 3 to 5 minutes. Transfer the fried mushrooms to the wire rack or towel-lined baking sheet and repeat with the remaining mushrooms.

6. Make the glaze: In a large bowl, whisk together the vegan butter, agave, lemon juice, lemon pepper, and black pepper until smooth.

7. Add the fried mushrooms to the bowl with the glaze and toss until thoroughly coated. Sprinkle with a pinch of lemon pepper and chopped parsley, and serve it up with some lemon wedges!

CELEBRATE!
Book club
meeting; low-key
wedding shower;
you finally get your
15 minutes of
fame!

Here comes your perfect high-low mash-up: If crab cakes and hush puppies had a baby, it would be this. Crab cakes, typically served at fancy-schmancy restaurants, don't feel like everyday food—they need a chill-mode update to become more relatable. Hush puppies, on the other hand, could use a glow-up—they're made with pantry ingredients and accompany many Southern meals, often served as a complimentary snack while you're scanning the menu. They're also a mainstay at any proper fish fry. These hush puppies definitely give me my crabby fix in one-bite form and are just as at home at casual fish fries as they are at dressier affairs.

crabby hush puppies

MAKES 12 TO 14 HUSH PUPPIES (SERVES 4)

4 cups **canola oil** or other neutral oil
½ cup **fine yellow cornmeal**
⅓ cup **all-purpose flour**
1½ teaspoons **granulated sugar**
1¼ teaspoons **Old Bay seasoning**
1 teaspoon **baking powder**

1 teaspoon **kosher salt**
⅛ teaspoon **cayenne pepper**
½ cup well-shaken **buttermilk**
1 large **egg white**
1 tablespoon **unsalted butter**, melted and cooled
8 ounces **claw crabmeat**, drained, flaked, and all cartilage removed

1 tablespoon minced **yellow onion**
2 teaspoons minced **fresh chives**
Finely chopped **fresh parsley leaves**, for serving (optional)

1. In a heavy-bottomed medium pot, heat the oil over medium-high heat until it registers 350°F on an instant-read thermometer. Line a large rimmed baking sheet with paper towels and set a wire rack on top.

2. In a medium bowl, whisk together the cornmeal, flour, sugar, Old Bay, baking powder, salt, and cayenne to combine. In a separate medium bowl, whisk together the buttermilk, egg white, and butter until combined. Stir in the crabmeat, onion, and chives until combined.

3. Add the wet ingredients to the dry ingredients and, using a spatula, stir to combine. In a batch, using a 1-ounce scooper or 2-tablespoon measure, gently drop balls of batter into the hot oil and fry until golden brown on all sides, turning halfway through frying, about 2 minutes total. Using a spider or slotted spoon, transfer the fried hush puppies to the prepared rack, let cool for 5 minutes, then serve, sprinkled with parsley (if using).

Maui is my favorite place on Earth. My connection to it is deep-deep. From my wedding (yep, I got Maui'd) to my babymoon to a random trip here and there, I always feel at peace as soon as I land on its exquisite soil. The clear azure waters still my spirit, the people reconnect me to joy, and the cuisine displays its heart in each bite. A recent visit led me to a restaurant called Kihei Caffe, where we devoured stacks of banana macadamia pancakes and loco moco, a local specialty in which a tender beef patty is drowned in rich brown gravy and served over white rice with a fried egg on top. Here I've replaced the rice with cheesy tater tots, making the ultimate Hawaiian breakfast into a can't-miss app.

hawaiian loco moco tatchos

SERVES 6

3 tablespoons **vegetable oil**, divided, plus more for greasing

1 (32-ounce) package **frozen tater tots**

1½ cups shredded **cheddar cheese**

8 ounces **80/20 ground beef**

1 small **yellow onion**, finely chopped and divided

2 small **garlic cloves**, minced or finely grated

3 teaspoons **soy sauce**, divided

1½ teaspoons **Worcestershire sauce**, divided

¾ teaspoon **kosher salt**, divided

1½ tablespoons **unsalted butter**, divided

4 ounces **cremini mushrooms**, stemmed and sliced

½ teaspoon **freshly ground black pepper**

½ teaspoon **garlic powder**

1½ tablespoons **all-purpose flour**

¾ cup **beef stock**

3 large **eggs**

¼ cup sliced **scallions**

1. Position a rack in the middle of the oven and preheat to 450°F. Lightly grease a large rimmed baking sheet with oil.

2. Spread the tots in an even layer on the prepared baking sheet. Bake for 20 to 25 minutes, until toasted through and golden brown. Remove from the oven and sprinkle with the cheese, then bake for 3 to 5 minutes more, until the cheese has melted. Remove from the oven and set aside.

3. Meanwhile, in a medium skillet, heat 1½ teaspoons of the oil over medium-high heat until shimmering. Add the beef, half of the onion, the garlic, 1½ teaspoons of the soy sauce, ¾ teaspoon of the Worcestershire, and ¼ teaspoon of the salt. Cook, breaking up the beef, until cooked through and no longer pink, 8 to 10 minutes. Using a slotted spoon, transfer the beef mixture to a large bowl and set aside.

recipe continues

4. Add the remaining 2½ tablespoons oil and ½ tablespoon of the butter to the same skillet. Add the mushrooms and the remaining onion and cook, stirring, until the mushrooms start to brown and the onion softens, 4 to 5 minutes. Season with the remaining ½ teaspoon salt, the pepper, and garlic powder and stir to combine.

5. Stir in the flour until thoroughly combined, then stir in the stock, the remaining 1½ teaspoons soy sauce, and the remaining ¾ teaspoon Worcestershire. Cook, stirring occasionally, until the sauce thickens and forms a gravy, 5 to 6 minutes. Return the beef mixture to the skillet and stir to combine with the mushrooms and gravy. Cook, stirring a few times, until warmed through, 3 to 5 minutes, then turn off the heat and let sit.

6. In a separate small skillet, melt the remaining 1 tablespoon butter over medium-high heat. Add the eggs and fry to your liking, sunny-side up or otherwise. Do you!

7. To serve, pour the beef and gravy over the tots, slide the fried eggs on top, and sprinkle with the scallions. Let your guests break the eggs into the tots and gravy and spoon portions onto their own plates. Yas!

CELEBRATE!
A fun summer luau in the backyard (make a few mai tais, roast a pig, and serve these!)

This is my ode to the salmon croquette, a Southern breakfast (or even dinner) essential where my mama reigns supreme. Her technique is simple: Grab canned salmon; add finely chopped veggies, seasonings, and a few binders; mix to combine; and press into patties. She then fries these patties up and serves them with buttermilk biscuits and syrup. For her, croquettes won't even get made if biscuits and syrup ain't on deck. Playing around with this family classic meant I needed to go big or go home and go big I did. I use roasted salmon in place of canned—this is great with leftover salmon, y'all. I add jerk flavors throughout and sneak in pureed mango to balance out the heat. Since these are a bit more elevated, you can forgo the biscuits if you want, but if biscuits are a must (I get it), the ones on page 30 are a lovely option.

jerk salmon croquettes

MAKES 10 CROQUETTES (SERVES 5)

5 tablespoons **Jerk Seasoning** (recipe follows) or store-bought, divided
2 teaspoons **smoked paprika**
½ teaspoon **cayenne pepper**
1 teaspoon **kosher salt**

1 pound **cooked salmon,** preferably wild-caught, skin removed (see Note)
½ cup cubed **mango**
Generous 2 tablespoons **fresh lime juice**
⅓ cup **plain bread crumbs**
¼ cup finely diced **yellow onion**

¼ cup finely diced **green bell pepper**
6 tablespoons **canola oil** or other neutral oil
½ cup **sour cream**
1 tablespoon minced **fresh chives**, plus more for serving
Lime wedges, for serving

1. Position a rack in the middle of the oven and preheat to 400°F. Line a large rimmed baking sheet with parchment paper.

2. In a small bowl, whisk together 3 tablespoons of the jerk seasoning, the paprika, cayenne, and salt until combined; set aside.

3. Set a bowl of water next to your workspace. In a large bowl, break the salmon into flakes. In a blender or mini food processor, combine the mango and lime juice and puree until smooth.

Add the mango-lime puree to the bowl with the salmon, then add the bread crumbs, onion, bell pepper, and jerk mixture and mix it on up with your hands to thoroughly combine. Form the salmon mixture into 2-inch-wide patties, moistening your hands with water to prevent the mixture from sticking. Place the shaped patties on a large plate as you work; you should get 10 patties.

recipe continues

4. In a large ovenproof skillet (preferably cast iron), heat the oil over medium-high heat until shimmering. Working in batches, if necessary, sear the patties until golden brown on the bottom, about 2 minutes. (If working in batches, transfer to a plate and repeat with the remaining patties, adding more oil to the pan between batches, if needed.) Flip the patties and transfer the skillet to the oven. Bake for about 7 minutes, until warmed through and golden brown on the bottom.

5. Meanwhile, in a medium bowl, stir together the sour cream, chives, and the remaining 2 tablespoons jerk seasoning. Serve the croquettes hot, with the seasoned sour cream for dipping, more chives, and lime wedges for squeezing over. The citrus just hits different.

note To cook salmon fresh for these croquettes, position a rack in the middle of the oven and preheat to 400°F. Lightly grease a large baking sheet with olive oil and place the salmon on it, skin-side down. Roast for 13 to 15 minutes, until the salmon is opaque and flakes easily with a fork. Remove from the oven and let cool completely before using for croquettes.

CELEBRATE!
Planning a fantasy—or real— vacation; special brunch; leftovers get to shine, too, boos!

jerk seasoning

I love making my own jerk seasoning—it takes just a few minutes to mix, and then you have it at the ready whenever the craving strikes or you need to be transported. Don't limit yourself to using it on seafood—try it on chicken or vegetables and imbue your dishes with flavor that will make you feel like you're on vacation. It's your world, boos! MAKES A GENEROUS ½ CUP

1½ tablespoons **garlic powder**
1½ tablespoons **dark brown sugar**
1 tablespoon **dried parsley**
2½ teaspoons **cayenne pepper**
2½ teaspoons **smoked paprika**
2 teaspoons **onion powder**
2 teaspoons **kosher salt**
1½ teaspoons **ground allspice**
1 teaspoon **freshly ground black pepper**
1 teaspoon **dried thyme**
½ teaspoon **ground cinnamon**
½ teaspoon **ground cumin**
½ teaspoon **freshly grated nutmeg**
¼ teaspoon **crushed red pepper flakes**

In a small bowl, whisk together the garlic powder, brown sugar, parsley, cayenne, paprika, onion powder, salt, allspice, black pepper, thyme, cinnamon, cumin, nutmeg, and red pepper flakes. Store in a lidded jar in a cool, dark place for up to 4 months.

I confess that I have a serious affinity for the show *Big Brother*. It started randomly a few years ago, and the next thing I knew, I watched every season. We all have those shows we never miss, chat about incessantly on Twitter, and join virtual leagues with other fans who understand our obsession (shout-out to my *Big Brother* FB chat group).

The beginning of each such season deserves epic party food. These crisp wings, glazed with a sweet-and-savory brown sugar sauce spiked with bourbon, understand the assignment.

bourbon-brown sugar wings

SERVES 4

CELEBRATE!
Premiere of your favorite show; NBA playoffs (I'm a big basketball fan, too); divorce party!

CHICKEN WINGS
2 teaspoons **baking powder**
2 teaspoons **garlic powder**
2 teaspoons **kosher salt**
1 teaspoon **freshly ground black pepper**
1 teaspoon **smoked paprika**
1 teaspoon **onion powder**
¼ teaspoon **cayenne pepper**, plus more to taste
2½ pounds **chicken wings**, tips removed, flats and drums separated

BOURBON-BROWN SUGAR SAUCE
1¾ cups packed **dark brown sugar**
¾ cup **bourbon**
2 tablespoons **tamari**
Generous 1 tablespoon **apple cider vinegar**
½ teaspoon **ground ginger**
½ teaspoon **cayenne pepper**
4 **garlic cloves**, minced or finely grated
2 tablespoons **unsalted butter**

1. **Make the chicken wings:** Position a rack in the middle of the oven and preheat to 425°F. Line a large rimmed baking sheet with parchment paper.

2. In a small bowl, whisk together the baking powder, garlic powder, salt, black pepper, paprika, onion powder, and cayenne until combined.

3. Thoroughly pat the chicken wings with paper towels until dry. Place the wings in a large bowl and sprinkle with half of the seasoning mixture. Flip the wings over and sprinkle with the remaining seasoning, then transfer them to the prepared baking sheet. Roast for 20 minutes, then remove from the oven, flip the wings, and roast for 25 minutes more, or until cooked through and crispy.

4. **Make the bourbon-brown sugar sauce:** In a medium pot, combine the brown sugar, bourbon, tamari, vinegar, ginger, cayenne, and garlic. Bring to a boil over medium-high heat, then reduce the heat to maintain a simmer and cook until the sauce thickly coats the back of a spoon, 5 to 8 minutes. Remove from the heat and whisk in the butter until completely incorporated.

5. Add the wings to the sauce and toss to evenly coat. Return the wings to the oven for 3 minutes more, so the sauce thickens and sticks to the wings—or 8 minutes if you want super-crispy wings—then remove from the oven and transfer to a platter. Serve right away and enjoy every saucy bite, boos!

VARIATIONS

For air-frying: Preheat an air fryer to 400°F. Spray the rack with cooking spray and arrange the chicken wings on the rack without over-crowding (you may need to do this in batches). Air-fry the wings for 15 to 17 minutes, flipping them halfway through cooking. Toss with the sauce and serve hot.

For grilling: Prepare a grill for direct heat. If using a gas grill, preheat to medium (350°F/175°C) with the lid closed, about 10 minutes. If using a charcoal grill, light the charcoal or wood briquettes; when the briquettes are white-hot and covered with ash, distribute them evenly over the cooking area. For a medium fire, you should be able to hold your hand about 6 inches above the coals for about 6 seconds. Have ready a spray bottle filled with water for taming any flames. Brush the grill grate with oil, if desired.

Grill the wings over indirect heat, turning occasionally to help slowly render the fat and cook the flesh without burning, for about 12 minutes, until the meat registers 165°F. To get char marks, place the wings over direct heat for 1 to 2 minutes before tossing with the sauce.

Give me a nugget of golden cornmeal-crusted deep-fried okra any day of the week! Okra can be one of those love-it-or-hate-it veggies (some just can't stand the slime, y'all!), but most Southern folk know it gets an invite to every party. Here I jazzed and remixed it a bit, because after a while, even fried okra wants to throw on a new outfit. Instead of your fresh-picked or even frozen variety, grab a jar of okra pickles—the preserved tangy fusion of vinegar and spices ups the ante. I fry those bad boys in a Japanese-style tempura batter, which makes them crisp and light. Lastly, a quick four-ingredient sauce (made with pantry staples you probably already have at the crib) balances it exquisitely. Get at it!

CELEBRATE!
Random friends drop over; condo association meeting (butter up the neighbors with these)

tempura-fried pickled okra

SERVES 6

TEMPURA
4 cups **vegetable oil**, for frying
¾ cup **cornstarch**
¾ cup **all-purpose flour**
1½ teaspoons **kosher salt**, plus more as needed
1½ cups cold **club soda**

2 large **eggs**, beaten
2 teaspoons **hot sauce**
2 (16-ounce) jars **okra pickles**, such as Wickles Wicked Okra pickles, drained
¼ cup chopped **scallions**

GARLIC-SOY MAYO
½ cup **mayonnaise**
2 tablespoons **soy sauce**
2 **garlic cloves**, minced or finely grated
¼ teaspoon **crushed red pepper flakes**

1. **Make the tempura:** In a 4-quart pot, heat the oil over medium heat until it registers 350°F on an instant-read thermometer. Line a large rimmed baking sheet with paper towels or a wire rack and keep it near your work area.

2. When the oil is close to being ready, in a large bowl, whisk together the cornstarch, flour, and salt until combined. Stir in the club soda, eggs, and hot sauce until just combined. Toss in the drained okra and stir to coat completely in the batter. Working in batches of 3 or 4 pieces, use tongs to lift the okra out of the batter, letting the excess drip back into the bowl, and gently add it to the hot oil. Fry the okra until light golden brown, 2 to 3 minutes total. Transfer to the prepared baking sheet and immediately season lightly with salt, boos.

3. **Make the garlic-soy mayo:** In a medium bowl, whisk together the mayonnaise, soy sauce, garlic, and red pepper flakes until combined. Serve the fried okra topped with the scallions and with the garlic-soy mayo for dipping.

Dancing has always made me forget everything that's stressing me out and lets me just "be." One of my favorite activities is throwing on '80s music videos and dancing with Harmony. Backed by Janet Jackson, Madonna, LL Cool J, and Eurythmics, we dance wildly as we sing into our pretend microphones. After our dance parties, we make appetizers like these fritters. I love the Southern pimiento cheese inspo I threw in the batter, along with the understated poblano pepper. Use fresh or frozen corn (it's your world, boos!). These flavorful patties can be handheld, so the party don't stop—fry these babies up and get back to the boogie.

pimiento cheese–poblano corn fritters

SERVES 4

1 medium **poblano pepper**

1 tablespoon **olive oil**, plus more as needed

1 cup **fresh or frozen corn kernels**, defrosted if frozen

¼ cup finely diced **yellow onion**

¼ cup finely diced **green bell pepper**

2 **garlic cloves**, minced or finely grated

Scant ½ cup **all-purpose flour**

1 tablespoon **fine yellow cornmeal**

1¾ teaspoons **granulated sugar**

½ teaspoon **baking powder**

½ teaspoon **kosher salt**

¼ teaspoon **cayenne pepper**

⅓ cup well-shaken **buttermilk**

1 large **egg**, lightly beaten

½ teaspoon **Worcestershire sauce**

¼ cup diced **pimiento peppers**, thoroughly drained

⅓ cup shredded **cheddar cheese**

Flaky sea salt, such as fleur de sel or Maldon

½ cup warmed **pepper jelly**, for serving (optional)

1. Preheat the broiler. Line a 9 by 13-inch rimmed baking sheet with aluminum foil.

2. Place the poblano on the prepared baking sheet and broil for 5 minutes on one side, or until the pepper starts to look super charred and almost blistered. Turn the pepper over and broil for 5 minutes more, or until blackened. Remove from the oven, transfer to a bowl, and cover the bowl with a plate. Let the poblano sit until cool to the touch, 5 to 10 minutes, then peel, seed, and dice the flesh.

3. In a medium skillet, heat the oil over medium heat until shimmering. Add the poblano, corn, onion, and bell pepper and cook, stirring, until softened, 4 to 5 minutes. Stir in the garlic and cook for an additional 30 seconds. Remove from the heat and set aside.

4. In a large bowl, whisk together the flour, cornmeal, sugar, baking powder, kosher salt, and cayenne until combined. In a small bowl, whisk together the buttermilk, egg, and Worcestershire until combined, then add the

CELEBRATE!
Impromptu
dance party, anyone?
Women Rock! Day
on January 3

wet ingredients to the dry ingredients and stir to create a thick batter. Fold in the cooked vegetables and pimientos until combined, then gently stir in the cheese and set aside for 10 minutes—this allows the batter to hydrate.

5. Pour enough oil into a large cast-iron skillet to just cover the bottom and heat over medium heat until shimmering. Working in batches, scoop 2 to 3 tablespoons of the batter into the skillet and spread each out like a small pancake, leaving 1 to 2 inches between each fritter. Fry until golden brown on the bottom, about 2 minutes, then flip and cook until golden brown on the other side, about 2 minutes more. Transfer to a paper towel–lined plate, immediately sprinkle with the flaky salt, and serve hot, with warm pepper jelly on the side, if you get down like that.

Y'all know laughing is best looking when the kitchen has good cooking! —*jocelyn*

salads & soups

Georgia Peach Salad with Candied Pecans and Cornbread Croutons *86*

'Tata Salad *89*

Watermelon Salad with Tomato, Pickled Onion, Mint, and Feta *90*

Winter Salad *93*

Lasagna Stew *96*

"Need a Hug" Sweet Potato Soup with Seared Scallops *99*

Cajun Seafood Chowder with Crispy Clams *101*

Mama's Chicken Soup for Ya Soul! *105*

This, my friends, is an ode to Georgia. My love affair with the Peach State began my first year at Clark Atlanta University. From historic institutions like Busy Bee Cafe and Paschal's, I was able to get my soul food fix. These restaurants became my home away from home, but nothing says Georgia like its undeniable peach game. Georgia peaches are luscious and juicy, and here the state fruit is the leading lady in a salad that honors her Southern charm.

georgia peach salad with candied pecans and cornbread croutons

SERVES 6

DRESSING
½ cup **extra-virgin olive oil**
Generous 1 tablespoon **honey**
Generous 1 tablespoon **balsamic vinegar**
Generous 1 tablespoon **fresh lemon juice**
1 small **shallot**, minced
½ teaspoon **crushed red pepper flakes**
½ teaspoon **kosher salt**
¼ teaspoon **freshly ground black pepper**

CROUTONS
3 cups cubed **leftover cornbread** (page 115 or your favorite recipe), at least 1 day old
2 tablespoons **extra-virgin olive oil**
Pinch of **kosher salt**

CANDIED PECANS
3 tablespoons packed **light brown sugar**
¼ teaspoon **kosher salt**
¼ teaspoon **ground cinnamon**
⅛ teaspoon **cayenne pepper**
1 cup **pecan halves**

SALAD
4 **ripe peaches** (about 1⅓ pounds total), halved, pitted, and sliced
1 **heirloom tomato**, halved and sliced
½ small **red onion**, sliced
3 cups **baby spinach**
1 ripe **avocado**, halved, pitted, and sliced
8 ounces **burrata cheese**
½ cup packed **fresh basil leaves**

1. **Make the dressing:** In a small bowl, whisk together the olive oil, honey, vinegar, lemon juice, shallot, red pepper flakes, salt, and black pepper until combined, then slide to the side.

2. **Make the croutons:** Position a rack in the middle of the oven and preheat to 400°F. Line a large rimmed baking sheet with parchment paper.

3. Spread the cornbread over the prepared baking sheet in one layer. Drizzle with the olive oil and sprinkle with the salt. Toast for about 15 minutes, stirring halfway, or until the cornbread cubes are a lovely deep brown color. Remove from the oven and let cool.

4. **Make the candied pecans:** Line a small rimmed baking sheet with parchment paper.

5. In a small skillet, whisk together the brown sugar, salt, cinnamon, cayenne, and 2 tablespoons water and bring to a simmer over medium heat. Add the pecans and cook, stirring continuously, until they're coated in the syrup, about 2 minutes. Transfer the pecans to the prepared baking sheet and spread them into a single layer. As the pecans cool, they will start to stick together (I get it! They are so delish, they can't get enough of each other!); once completely cooled, break them apart.

6. **Make the salad:** In a large bowl, toss the peaches, tomato, and onion with 2 teaspoons of the dressing and let sit for a few minutes.

7. When you're ready to serve, put the spinach in a serving dish or on a platter, then place the marinated peach mixture and the sliced avocado on top. Tear the burrata and place it in the center, then top with the croutons, basil leaves, and ½ cup of the candied pecans (see Note). Drizzle with the remaining dressing and serve.

note You'll have about ½ cup of candied pecans left over. Use them to make more salad, garnish your morning oatmeal, or just snack on 'em, boos!

CELEBRATE!
Juneteenth; the ultimate cookout; summer dinner partay

CELEBRATE!
All cookouts;
something great
to make with
ingredients you
already have

"Who made the potato salad?" might be the most controversial question for Black folks. If you are lucky enough to be invited to the cookout, the potato salad will be its centerpiece. While the Culture may disagree on which way to make it (mayo vs. Miracle Whip, celery vs. celery seed, chunky vs. creamy), we agree on its importance. My cousin Johnnie Mae makes one so damn good, it's requested at various family functions. Her rules are: First, don't overcook the potatoes. Second, Johnnie doesn't measure her seasonings, letting the ancestors guide each pinch and sprinkle instead, which made writing this recipe calculus-level difficult. (I took a few liberties with it and the fam still loved it.) And finally, if you get asked to make the 'tata salad, treat it with the utmost respect. Folks get downright clowned and disinvited if they screw it up.

'tata salad

SERVES 8 TO 10

2½ pounds **white potatoes** (about 6 medium), peeled and cut into ½-inch cubes

¾ cup **mayonnaise**, such as Duke's

½ cup finely chopped **whole sweet baby pickles** (about 6 pickles), plus ½ cup **pickle brine** from the jar

2 tablespoons **yellow mustard**

1½ tablespoons **granulated sugar**, plus more to taste

1 teaspoon **white vinegar** or apple cider vinegar

¾ teaspoon **seasoned salt**, such as Lawry's, plus more to taste

½ teaspoon **celery salt**, plus more to taste

½ teaspoon **freshly ground black pepper**, plus more to taste

¼ teaspoon **Accent seasoning** or MSG

5 **hard-boiled eggs**

Sweet paprika, for garnish

1. Place the potatoes in a large pot and add water to cover. Bring the water to a boil over high heat and cook until the potatoes are fork-tender, 10 to 15 minutes. Don't overcook them, boos—you don't want them to be too mushy. Drain the potatoes and rinse under cold running water for about 30 seconds, then set aside to drain and cool completely.

2. In a large bowl, whisk together the mayonnaise, pickles, pickle brine, mustard, sugar, vinegar, seasoned salt, celery salt, pepper, and Accent until combined. Very finely chop 4 of the hard-boiled eggs and add them to the bowl, followed by the potatoes. Gently fold until the ingredients are thoroughly combined.

3. Taste and adjust the seasonings according to your taste buds, my friends. It's your world! Serve at room temperature or cover and refrigerate until needed. When ready to serve, sprinkle paprika over the salad, then slice the remaining egg and fan it out over the top.

One of my favorite books is *The Bluest Eye* by Toni Morrison. It truly drops knowledge on eye-opening (pun intended) subject matter: Black female identity and self-love. Black women have consistently struggled with acknowledging our beauty because society hasn't always lauded our allure. Black girl magic can be downright ignored, but in Morrison's book, it's front and center. I would not be who I am today without the generations of strong Black women. Visionaries, creators, and everyday geniuses like my Big Mama paved the way. Today when I think about my queens, from my sister-friends to my sorors of Alpha Kappa Alpha Sorority, Inc., I'm surrounded by the exquisiteness others have found unworthy.

Why am I talking about this in the headnote for a watermelon salad? Watermelon, despite its historic significance in my African heritage, has been stigmatized by white America and associated with insensitive, shaming stereotypes. A lot of my people won't even eat watermelon around white folks—racism has made us resent and diminish the significance, beauty, and nutrition of watermelon, even though it's a symbol of our rich history. But I think it's time to reclaim it. As my friend Toni Tipton-Martin wrote in her famed cookbook *Jubilee*, "Our cooking, our cooks, shall be free from caricature and stereotype. We have earned the freedom to cook with creativity and joy." Amen.

watermelon salad with tomato, pickled onion, mint, and feta

SERVES 4

PICKLED ONION
1 cup **white vinegar**
¼ cup **granulated sugar**
2 teaspoons **kosher salt**
1 cup very thinly sliced **red onion**
1 **garlic clove**, peeled

CHIPOTLE DRESSING
1 tablespoon **extra-virgin olive oil**
2 tablespoons minced **shallot**
⅓ cup **fresh lime juice** or orange juice or a mix

2 tablespoons **red wine vinegar**
2 tablespoons **honey**
1 tablespoon **Dijon mustard**
1 canned **chipotle pepper in adobo sauce**
¾ teaspoon **kosher salt**
¼ teaspoon **freshly ground black pepper**

SALAD
4 cups cubed **seedless watermelon**
2 cups chopped **heirloom tomatoes**

1 cup **fresh arugula**
½ cup torn **fresh mint leaves**, plus more if needed for serving
½ cup torn **fresh basil leaves**
1 medium **cucumber**, chopped
½ small **fennel bulb**, very thinly sliced
½ cup crumbled **feta cheese**

recipe continues

1. Make the pickled onion: In a medium pot, combine the vinegar, sugar, salt, and 1 cup water and heat over medium-high heat, stirring, until the sugar and salt have completely dissolved, about 2 minutes. Remove from the heat and let cool to room temperature.

2. Put the onion and garlic in a 2-cup mason jar or other container with a lid, then pour the pickling liquid over, close, and chill-mode in the fridge for at least 2 hours. (The onion's purple color will fade with time and tint the pickling liquid—this is completely on point.)

3. Make the dressing: In a small pan, heat the oil over medium heat until shimmering. Add the shallot and cook, stirring, until softened, about 3 minutes. Remove from the heat and transfer to a food processor. Add the lime juice, vinegar, honey, mustard, chipotle, salt, and black pepper. Pulse until thoroughly combined, then transfer to a lidded jar and slide to the side. You should have about ¾ cup dressing.

4. Make the salad: In a large bowl, toss together the watermelon, tomatoes, arugula, mint, basil, cucumber, and fennel until combined. Drizzle the salad with ¼ cup of the dressing and gently toss again. Taste and add more dressing as needed, tossing to incorporate. Sprinkle with the pickled onion, feta, and additional mint, if desired, and serve immediately.

CELEBRATE! Juneteenth (we often include red foods, which signify the blood shed during the slave trade)

Dance classes ruled my life until my early twenties. In addition to ballet, pointe, jazz, tap, lyrical, and hip-hop classes, I was also a member of New Life Performance Company, a liturgical community theater troupe of about forty teenagers who performed in churches and throughout the Chicago area and even traveled nationally. New Life was founded by my mentor Anthony Hollins, a treasure of a human being. Zany, bubbly, hilarious, and insanely talented, Anthony was also an HIV awareness activist. Anthony inspired and demanded the best from all of us, pushing us to be better, despite our youth.

One night, when I was thirteen, he shared with us that he was living with AIDS. We had all heard about the AIDS epidemic, but he was the first person I personally knew with the virus. Our troupe continued to dance together for years, and when Anthony passed away in 2007 at the age of forty-two, we reunited to dance at his funeral. I still deeply feel his impact on my life, an impact few others have matched.

While he was alive, Anthony reminded us to eat for energy and health, and I take this to heart to this day. This winter salad, with acorn squash, apple, and pomegranate seeds, is nutritious, colorful, and vibrant, reminding me of Anthony's spirit.

winter salad

SERVES 6

SQUASH
½ cup (1 stick) **unsalted butter**
2 tablespoons **Calabrian chile paste** or sriracha
½ teaspoon **kosher salt**
½ teaspoon **freshly ground black pepper**
½ teaspoon **garlic powder**
½ teaspoon **ground cumin**
¼ teaspoon **smoked paprika**
1 **acorn squash** or delicata squash, halved lengthwise, seeded, and sliced into ¼-inch-thick half-moons

ORANGE-GINGER BUTTERMILK DRESSING
¾ cup **sour cream**
½ cup well-shaken **whole-milk buttermilk**
1½ tablespoons finely grated **orange zest**
2 teaspoons minced **fresh ginger**
1½ teaspoons **kosher salt**
1 teaspoon minced **fresh flat-leaf parsley**
¾ teaspoon **freshly ground black pepper**
¼ teaspoon **garlic powder**

SALAD
2 cups chopped stemmed **kale leaves**
2 cups **tricolor slaw mix**
1 medium **red apple**, cored and diced small
Seeds from 1 small **pomegranate** (about 1½ cups)

recipe continues

1. **Roast the squash:** Position a rack in the middle of the oven and preheat to 400°F. Line a large rimmed baking sheet with parchment paper.

2. In a small nonstick skillet, melt the butter over medium heat. Cook, stirring with a wooden spoon or silicone spatula, until the butter solids are brown and smell nutty, 4 to 5 minutes. Remove from the heat and stir in the chile paste, salt, pepper, garlic powder, cumin, and paprika. Add the squash and gently toss or stir to coat with the spiced butter, then transfer to the prepared baking sheet. Roast the squash for about 40 minutes, until tender and golden, flipping the slices halfway through. Remove from the oven and let cool completely.

3. **Make the dressing:** In a medium bowl, whisk together the sour cream, buttermilk, orange zest, ginger, salt, parsley, pepper, and garlic powder until well combined.

4. **Assemble the salad:** When ready to serve, in a large bowl, toss together the kale, slaw mix, and apple until combined. Transfer to a serving platter and top with the squash and pomegranate seeds. Drizzle with the dressing and serve it up, boos.

CELEBRATE!
Honoring a deceased loved one; your first dance class!

Lasagna is one of my all-time favorite meals, and to me it tastes like love personified. It takes a long time to put together, and why would you do that for someone you didn't completely love? You don't make lasagna for just anyone. Each bite has a sense of care, technique, effort, and emotion. This kind of time commitment also means that lasagna is a special-occasion meal. Well, I wanted to have lasagna more often, so I thought of a simpler option that could just warm up your spirits whenever you needed it, even on a weeknight.

lasagna stew

SERVES 8

CELEBRATE!
Meeting "the one";
baby taking their first
steps; nailing an
audition

- 4 tablespoons **extra-virgin olive oil**, divided, plus more as needed
- 1 pound **ground chicken sausage**, casings removed
- 1 pound **ground turkey**, preferably dark meat
- 1 medium **yellow onion**, diced
- 1 medium **green bell pepper**, seeded and diced
- 7 **garlic cloves**, minced or finely grated
- 1 (28-ounce) can **crushed tomatoes**

- 1 (14-ounce) can **tomato sauce**
- 1 (6-ounce) can **tomato paste**
- 2 cups **chicken stock**
- ¼ cup **red wine**
- 2 tablespoons **Italian Seasoning** (page 64) or store-bought
- 1 tablespoon **granulated sugar**, plus more to taste
- 2 teaspoons **kosher salt**, plus more as needed
- 1 teaspoon **freshly ground black pepper**, plus more to taste

- 8 **lasagna noodles** or 7 ounces pappardelle, broken into ¾-inch-wide strips/pieces
- Shredded **mozzarella cheese**, for serving
- Grated **Parmesan cheese**, for serving
- **Ricotta cheese**, for serving
- Handful of **fresh basil**, chopped, for serving
- Handful of chopped **fresh flat-leaf parsley**, for serving
- **Crushed red pepper flakes**, for serving

1. In a large pot, heat 3 tablespoons of the olive oil over medium heat until shimmering. Add the sausage and turkey and cook, stirring and breaking up the meat with a wooden spoon, until no longer pink, about 5 minutes. Using a slotted spoon, transfer the meat to a bowl and slide to the side.

2. Add the remaining 1 tablespoon olive oil to the pot, followed by the onion and bell pepper, and cook, stirring, until the onion softens and becomes translucent, about 3 minutes. Add

the garlic and cook until that bomb aroma fills the kitchen, about 30 seconds, then return the meat and any accumulated juices from the bowl to the pot.

3. Add the crushed tomatoes, tomato sauce, tomato paste, stock, wine, Italian seasoning, sugar, salt, and black pepper and stir to combine. Bring the mixture to a simmer, then lower the heat and simmer, stirring occasionally, until the stew thickens up a bit, about 25 minutes.

4. Meanwhile, bring a medium pot of water to a boil. Add enough salt so the water tastes like the sea, then cook the noodles until al dente according to the package instructions. Drain, toss with a drizzle of oil to prevent sticking, and set aside.

5. Taste the stew and season with more sugar, salt, and/or black pepper, if needed. Add the pasta to the stew and stir to combine. Ladle the stew into bowls and top with the mozzarella, Parmesan, ricotta, basil, parsley, and red pepper flakes. Serve hot and get at it.

The day I found out my father had bone cancer, I sat in the car and cried. Then I dried my tears, began healing affirmations, ordered a bowl of soup, ate it in the car, and drove to see him. To my surprise, he was incredibly optimistic and outlined his doctor's plan with such certainty that my mindset immediately shifted to positivity as well.

That bowl of soup was the hug I needed in that moment of despair. I think of this soup, dressed up here with seared scallops, as the ideal meal for when you need an emotional pick-me-up.

"need a hug" sweet potato soup with seared scallops

SERVES 4 TO 6

SOUP
2 tablespoons **extra-virgin olive oil**, plus more as needed
1 medium **yellow onion**, chopped
4 **garlic cloves**, chopped
2 large **sweet potatoes** (2 pounds total), peeled and diced
1 cup chopped **cauliflower**
Kosher salt and **freshly ground black pepper**

3 cups **low-sodium chicken stock**
1 cup **light coconut milk**
1 tablespoon **maple syrup**
1 teaspoon packed **light brown sugar**
1 teaspoon **yellow curry powder**
½ teaspoon **ground ginger**
¼ teaspoon **smoked paprika**, plus more as needed

SCALLOPS
1 pound fresh large **sea scallops**
3 slices **thick-cut bacon**, chopped
1 large **shallot**, diced
No-Salt Cajun Seasoning (page 37) or store-bought
Kosher salt
1 tablespoon **extra-virgin olive oil**
Smoked paprika, for dusting
Fresh flat-leaf parsley, for garnish

1. Make the soup: In a large stockpot, heat the oil over medium-high heat until shimmering. Add the onion and cook, stirring, until tender and starting to brown, 5 to 6 minutes. Stir in the garlic and cook until aromatic, about 30 seconds. Adjust the heat if the onion and garlic begin to burn. Add the sweet potatoes and cauliflower, season with salt and pepper, and cook until both are slightly softened, about 5 minutes. If the bottom of the pot starts to look dry, add more olive oil as needed.

recipe continues

2. Add the stock and coconut milk and stir to combine. Stir in the maple syrup, brown sugar, curry powder, ginger, and paprika until combined. Bring to a simmer, then reduce the heat to low, cover, and cook until the sweet potatoes and cauliflower are tender and easily pierced with a fork, about 25 minutes.

3. Remove from the heat and, using an immersion blender, carefully puree the soup until completely smooth. (Alternatively, let the soup cool a bit, then transfer it to a standing blender in batches, puree, and return the blended soup to the pot.)

4. Return the soup to medium-low heat and cook until thickened, 7 to 9 minutes. Taste and season with more salt, pepper, and/or paprika, if desired. Cover and keep warm while you prepare the scallops.

5. Make the scallops: Line a rimmed baking sheet with paper towels and set the scallops on top. Cover with more paper towels and press gently to absorb the extra moisture. We want these babies dry as a bone for a lovely sear. Set aside for 10 minutes.

6. In a large skillet, combine the bacon and shallot and cook over medium-high heat, stirring continuously, until the bacon is cooked through and the shallot is tender and starting to color, 6 to 7 minutes. Transfer the bacon and shallot to a small bowl.

7. Liberally sprinkle the scallops on both sides with Cajun seasoning and salt. In the same skillet you used for the bacon, heat the oil over medium-high heat. Add the scallops in a single layer (depending on the size of your skillet, you may need to cook them in batches) and sear until browned on both sides, 1½ to 2 minutes per side.

8. To serve, ladle the soup into bowls and sprinkle with a dusting of paprika. Gently place several scallops on top of the soup in each bowl (dividing them evenly)—they may or may not sink, which is fine either way—spoon some bacon and shallot over the top, and garnish with the parsley.

CELEBRATE!
Self-care day
(each spoonful
is like a warm hug—
perfect!)

I'm what you would call a Daddy's girl. He still calls me Princess, and he's my absolute hero. If anyone in my family wants to convince Daddy to do something, they ask me to talk to him about it. I also inherited his food passions, especially seafood. When I was younger and spent my summers working for his dental practice, he'd take me to seafood restaurants for lunch. We'd feast on everything from flounder, whiting, grouper, and perch to smelt, buffalo fish, and crappie. But our favorite is a good bowl of chowder, so this recipe is a love letter to Dad and our shared love of seafood. It is filled with textures and flavor and can be adapted to whatever seafood is freshest or available to you.

cajun seafood chowder with crispy clams

SERVES 6 TO 8

CHOWDER
2 slices **thick-cut bacon** or 4 ounces **pancetta**, chopped small

5 tablespoons **unsalted butter**, divided

½ cup finely chopped **onion**

½ cup finely chopped **green bell pepper**

¼ cup finely chopped **celery**

2 teaspoons **No-Salt Cajun Seasoning** (page 37) or store-bought, divided

½ teaspoon **kosher salt**, plus more to taste

4 **garlic cloves**, minced or finely grated

3 tablespoons **all-purpose flour**

2 cups **chicken stock** or seafood stock, divided

2 (10-ounce) cans chopped **clams**, drained, liquid reserved

1 pound **Yukon Gold potatoes** or Japanese sweet potatoes, peeled and cut into ½-inch cubes

1 cup **half-and-half**

Large pinch of **saffron**

¼ teaspoon **cayenne pepper**

1 pound **fresh cod**, chopped into medium chunks

8 ounces **cooked lobster meat**, chopped into medium chunks

CRISPY CLAMS
Nonstick cooking spray

1 large **egg**, beaten

1 teaspoon **half-and-half**

Pinch of **kosher salt**

¼ cup **rice flour**

¼ cup **fine yellow cornmeal**

¼ teaspoon **No-Salt Cajun Seasoning** (page 37) or store-bought

¼ teaspoon **freshly ground black pepper**

1 (10-ounce) can **whole baby clams**, drained

TO SERVE
Chopped **fresh flat-leaf parsley**

Pinch of **Aleppo pepper** (optional)

Oyster crackers (optional)

recipe continues

1. **Make the chowder:** In a large pot, cook the bacon over medium heat until the fat starts to render and the meat starts to brown slightly, 2 to 3 minutes. Add 2 tablespoons of the butter and let it melt, then add the onion, bell pepper, and celery and cook, stirring frequently, until the vegetables are tender, about 3 minutes. Stir in 1 teaspoon of the Cajun seasoning and the salt. Stir in the garlic and cook until aromatic, about 30 seconds. Stir in the all-purpose flour and cook until incorporated, about 1 minute.

2. Add ¾ cup of the stock, stirring it aggressively into the mixture in the pot, then bring to a simmer. Add the remaining 1 teaspoon Cajun seasoning, the reserved clam liquid, and the remaining 1¼ cups stock. Add the potatoes, half-and-half, remaining 3 tablespoons butter, the saffron, and cayenne and stir to combine. Bring to a boil, then reduce the heat to medium-low, cover, and cook until the potatoes are tender, 15 to 20 minutes.

3. Add the clams, cod, and lobster meat, cover, and turn off the heat. (If using an electric stove, remove the pot from the burner and set aside.) Let the residual heat cook the seafood until the cod flakes easily with a fork, about 10 minutes. Taste and season with more salt, if desired.

4. **Make the crispy clams:** Preheat an air fryer to 400°F. Lightly spray the basket of the air fryer with the cooking spray.

5. In a small bowl, whisk together the egg, half-and-half, and salt until combined. In another small bowl, whisk together the rice flour, cornmeal, Cajun seasoning, and black pepper. Dip the clams in the egg mixture, letting the excess drip back in the bowl, then dredge them in the flour mixture. Working in batches to avoid overcrowding, add the clams to the air fryer basket and liberally spray their tops with cooking spray.

6. Air-fry for 4 to 5 minutes, until golden brown on the bottom, then gently flip the clams and spray with cooking spray. Air-fry for 1 to 2 minutes more, until golden brown on the outside but still juicy and tender on the inside. Transfer the clams to a wire rack and let cool for about 3 minutes.

7. Ladle the chowder into bowls and top with the fried clams. Garnish with parsley and Aleppo pepper, if desired, and serve with oyster crackers on the side, if you like. Dig into that, boos.

CELEBRATE!
Seafood feast; completion of a goal; National Soup It Forward Day (March 3)

CELEBRATE!
When your spirits
need a lil' lifting;
a snowy day deserves
a bowl of this
comfort

Growing up in Chicago, where winters are brutally cold, I looked forward to my mama's weekly batch of this creamy and comforting soup. I was also really into James Canfield's Chicken Soup for the Soul book series, where I found inspiring stories of people just like me who overcame adversity and reached higher despite dire circumstances. Later in life, I deeply connected with James's philosophies regarding the laws of attraction and manifesting the life I truly wanted. His book *The Success Principles* helped me understand that this life wasn't dependent on things outside of me. These days, I still love the genius behind the title—chicken soup nourishes your belly while lifting your spirits—and I beg Mama to make this soup for me, because I never feel better than after a bowl of it.

mama's chicken soup for ya soul!
SERVES 8 TO 12

Meat from 1 (3-pound) **rotisserie chicken**, shredded
2 (10.5-ounce) cans **cream of chicken soup**, such as Campbell's
1 large **white onion**, finely chopped
½ cup (1 stick) **unsalted butter**

1½ tablespoons **chicken bouillon**, such as Better Than Bouillon
1 tablespoon **granulated sugar**
2 teaspoons **freshly ground black pepper**
1 teaspoon **garlic powder**
1 teaspoon **seasoned salt**, such as Lawry's

5 medium **carrots**, finely chopped
3 **celery stalks**, finely diced
Kosher salt
1 pound **wide egg noodles**
2 tablespoons **olive oil**
⅓ cup chopped **fresh flat-leaf parsley**, for serving (optional)

1. Place the shredded chicken in a large stockpot. Add the canned soup, onion, butter, bouillon, sugar, pepper, garlic powder, and seasoned salt. Cover with 6 cups water and stir. Bring to a boil over medium-high heat, then reduce the heat to medium, cover, and cook, stirring occasionally, until the stock thickens and the flavors meld, about 45 minutes. That stock gets good, y'all.

2. Add the carrots and celery, along with 3 cups water. Raise the heat to medium-high and bring the soup to a boil. Reduce the heat to medium-low, cover, and cook until the vegetables are tender, 15 to 20 minutes. Turn off the heat and let the soup hang out for 10 to 15 minutes; it will continue to thicken as it sits.

3. Meanwhile, bring a large pot of salted water to a boil. Add the egg noodles and cook until al dente according to package instructions. Drain and transfer to a large bowl. Toss with the olive oil and set aside.

4. When ready to serve, ladle the soup into bowls, add however much noodles you desire (do you, boos!), and garnish with the parsley, if using.

There's nothing more special than love shared over some mac and cheese. —*jocelyn*

side dishes

Mac and cheese in Black culture is as obligatory—if not more—as turkey on Thanksgiving. While my culture isn't monolithic, we largely agree that learning to make mac and cheese is a rite of passage with the following requirements. One: It's baked, period, full stop. We don't stovetop in these streets. The top must be golden and bubbling and boast a crust of melty cheeses. Two: Several cheeses must be used to result in a flavor bomb. Three: While my people may differ on whether to use eggs or a béchamel-based sauce, the result must be creamy yet casserole-y. Cheese pulls should ensue. When you make this recipe, adapted from my auntie Rose, you will likely become the family's designated mac-and-cheese maker, the truest honor of them all—you've been warned. *PHOTOGRAPH ON PAGE 106*

THE ultimate mac and cheese

SERVES 8 TO 10

1 **chicken bouillon cube,** such as Knorr

1 pound **large elbow pasta**

1½ cups shredded **sharp cheddar cheese**

1½ cups shredded **mild cheddar cheese**

1½ cups shredded **Colby Jack** or pepper Jack cheese (for a kick)

1½ cups shredded **Gruyère cheese**

1 cup shredded **mozzarella cheese**

4 tablespoons (½ stick) **unsalted butter**

¼ cup **all-purpose flour**

2 teaspoons **garlic powder**

1½ teaspoons **onion powder**

2 teaspoons **kosher salt**

1 teaspoon **freshly ground black pepper**

¾ teaspoon **smoked paprika**

½ teaspoon **mustard powder**

½ teaspoon **granulated sugar**

¼ teaspoon **freshly grated nutmeg**

⅛ teaspoon **cayenne pepper**

2½ cups **heavy cream**

2½ cups **whole milk**

½ cup **sour cream**

1½ teaspoons **Worcestershire sauce**

1 teaspoon **hot sauce**

3 tablespoons minced **fresh chives,** for serving

1. Fill a large heavy-bottomed pot with 5 quarts water and bring to a boil over high heat. Add the bouillon cube and stir to dissolve. Add the pasta and cook until al dente according to the package instructions. Drain the pasta and slide to the side.

2. Position a rack in the middle of the oven and preheat to 375°F.

3. In a large bowl, toss together the cheddars, Colby Jack, Gruyère, and mozzarella until combined.

4. In a large heavy-bottomed pot, melt the butter over medium heat. Whisk in the flour and cook, whisking continuously, to form a roux, about 1 minute. Whisk in the garlic powder, onion powder, salt, black pepper, paprika, mustard powder, sugar, nutmeg, and cayenne until incorporated. Whisk in the heavy cream, milk, sour cream, Worcestershire, and hot sauce until combined and let the sour cream completely melt into the sauce. Whisk in half the shredded cheese mixture and let it melt completely into creamy deliciousness, whisking all the while. Whisk until the sauce thickens a bit, about 3 minutes, then add the drained pasta and stir to evenly coat it in the sauce.

5. Transfer a third of the pasta mixture to a 9 by 13 by 2-inch baking pan and top with a third of the remaining cheese mixture, then repeat two more times, finishing with the cheese. Bake for 40 to 45 minutes, until the pasta is golden brown in places and the sauce is bubbling. Remove from the oven and let cool for 10 minutes, then garnish with chives and serve hot. May the cheese pulls be ever in your favor.

Consider me the ultimate fan of all things potatoes. They soothe my soul unlike any other food, whether baked, in chip form (don't judge), or a massive bowl of buttery mashed potatoes that I like to eat alone while watching *This Is Us* (again, don't judge). These wedges, inspired by the Greek medley of lemon, garlic, oregano, and rosemary, are a fam favorite. They're fantastic for entertaining or for a solo supper. The wedges crisp up perfectly in the oven but that sauce—OMG—is crazy! I drizzle it on the potatoes for over-the-top flavor and finish with a shower of crumbled feta.

crispy greek lemon potato wedges

SERVES 4

CELEBRATE!
Rainy day that deserves a cozy; solo dinner (ain't nothin' wrong with eating just potatoes for dinner)

¼ cup **olive oil**, plus more for brushing

4 tablespoons (½ stick) **unsalted butter**, melted

¼ cup **fresh lemon juice**

¼ cup **chicken stock**

2 teaspoons **kosher salt**

1 tablespoon **dried oregano**

1 tablespoon chopped **fresh rosemary**, plus a few sprigs for garnish

½ teaspoon **freshly ground black pepper**

½ teaspoon **smoked paprika**

4 medium **russet potatoes** (3½ pounds), cut into ¾-inch-thick wedges

7 **garlic cloves**, minced or finely grated (about 2 tablespoons)

½ cup crumbled **feta cheese**

¼ cup chopped **fresh flat-leaf parsley**

1. Position a rack in the middle of the oven and preheat to 425°F. Lightly brush a large rimmed baking sheet with a little olive oil.

2. In a large bowl, whisk together the olive oil, butter, lemon juice, stock, salt, oregano, rosemary, pepper, and paprika until combined. Add the potatoes and toss until thoroughly coated.

3. Transfer the potatoes to the prepared baking sheet (reserve that magic lemon sauce in the bowl) and spread them out evenly into a single layer. Roast for about 20 minutes, until easily pierced with a paring knife. Remove the potatoes from the oven, stir in the garlic, and

roast the potatoes for 20 to 30 minutes more, until golden brown and incredibly crispy.

4. While the potatoes are roasting, transfer the reserved lemon sauce to a small saucepan and bring to a boil over medium heat. Reduce the heat to low and simmer until the sauce has thickened, 5 to 7 minutes. Remove from the heat and keep warm.

5. Once the potatoes are ready, transfer them to a serving platter and immediately shower them with the feta and parsley. Drizzle with the sauce, garnish with the rosemary sprigs, and serve right away, with the remaining sauce alongside for additional drizzling.

In many Black families, grits are as ubiquitous as salt and pepper. When I was growing up, there was not a breakfast without grits. Sometimes I just want a bowl of grits for dinner, so I make them for me and my husband. I've never had a complaint—that's good eatin'! Here I elevate this humble food to something really special. Instead of making the grits on the stovetop, I tuck them into a gooey, creamy bake, almost like a casserole. It's a delicious side at a weekend supper, holiday table, or festive brunch. But to be honest, it's terrific all on its own.

gooey baked cheesy grits

SERVES 6

4 cups (1 quart) **chicken stock**
Kosher salt
1 cup **old-fashioned grits**
Bacon grease or vegetable oil, for greasing
4 tablespoons (½ stick) **salted butter**, cut into pieces

Generous ⅓ cup coarsely grated **cheddar cheese**
2 tablespoons finely grated **Parmesan cheese**, plus more for topping
2 small **garlic cloves**, minced or finely grated

¼ teaspoon **garlic powder**
1 cup **whole milk** or half-and-half
2 large **eggs**, beaten
Chopped **fresh thyme** or flat-leaf parsley, for serving (optional)

1. In a medium pot, bring the stock to a boil over medium-high heat and season to taste with salt. The stock should taste assertively seasoned but not overly salty. Whisk the grits into the boiling stock, then reduce the heat to the lowest setting, cover, and cook until the grits are tender and thickened but still pourable, 15 to 18 minutes, stirring once halfway through cooking.

2. While the grits are cooking, position a rack in the middle of the oven and preheat to 325°F. Grease a large 2-quart/9 by 13 by 2-inch baking dish with bacon grease.

3. Remove the grits from the heat and whisk in the butter, cheddar, Parmesan, garlic, and garlic powder until the cheeses and butter have completely melted and the ingredients

are thoroughly combined. Whisk in the milk, then whisk in the eggs until incorporated.

4. Transfer the grits to the prepared baking dish, then sprinkle with Parmesan cheese. Bake for 1 hour 15 minutes to 1 hour 25 minutes, until the grits are browned around the edges, starting to pull away from the sides of the baking dish, and wiggle just slightly in the center when you shake the dish. If you want a rich brown top, you can slide the grits under the broiler for 4 to 5 minutes, until the cheese is bubbling and golden.

5. Sprinkle the grits with the thyme (if using) and serve.

If you've eaten enough cornbread, chances are you're aware of the sweet-versus-savory camps, neither willing to admit there's more than one way to make cornbread. I grew up eating a savory skillet version served alongside greens. At some point in my childhood, my mom (the family rebel) introduced us to Jiffy, and we switched to Team Sweet. These days, I believe there's room for both kinds of cornbread. This recipe, with browned butter for nutty notes, straddles both worlds and makes you want to eat the entire skillet in one sitting. I prefer to coat the pan with bacon grease, which I always have on hand (y'all, I was raised up right!), or shortening. But if you only have oil or butter, that's fine, too.

honeychile brown butter cornbread

SERVES 8

CELEBRATE!
Thanksgiving; prefinals meal, because you could use a bit more luck

4 tablespoons (½ stick/ 57 grams) **salted butter**
1 cup (125 grams) **all-purpose flour**
1 cup (160 grams) **medium or fine cornmeal**

¼ cup (50 grams) **granulated sugar**
1 tablespoon **baking powder**
1 cup (225 grams) well-shaken **buttermilk**
⅓ cup (112 grams) **honey**

¼ cup (50 grams) **canola oil** or vegetable oil
2 large **eggs**, at room temperature
1 teaspoon **vanilla extract**
Bacon grease or shortening, for greasing

1. Position a rack in the middle of the oven and preheat to 400°F.

2. In a small saucepan, melt the butter over medium heat and cook until it begins to brown and tiny flecks of nuttiness develop, about 4 minutes, being careful not to let it burn. Remove from the heat and let cool until warm to the touch.

3. In a large bowl, whisk together the flour, cornmeal, sugar, and baking powder until combined. In a separate medium bowl, whisk together the buttermilk, honey, oil, eggs,

vanilla, and the cooled brown butter. Add the wet ingredients to the dry ingredients and mix until well combined; set aside.

4. Thoroughly grease a 10-inch cast-iron skillet with bacon grease and place it in the oven to heat for 4 to 5 minutes. Transfer the skillet to a heatproof surface and pour in the batter. Bake for 20 to 25 minutes, until the top is crisp and golden brown.

5. Transfer to a wire rack and let cool slightly, then serve straight from the skillet.

Finding Black women in my industry is harder than you might think. A group of us started connecting weekly over Zoom, and after about a year of virtual meetings, we planned a retreat in Mexico City. We wanted authentic experiences and to avoid the touristy stuff: We got to make tacos over a wood fire and learned our guide's grandmother's salsa recipe, made in a generational molcajete. Each experience brought us closer and provided us with the most incredible food. Simple, honest Mexican flavors that came together in homey, traditional dishes felt just like home, even though I didn't grow up eating the exact same foods. All goes to show you we have far more in common than we might think. I grew up eating corn pudding and this take was inspired by my trip and the flavors of the elote I ate in Mexico City.

elote fried corn pudding

SERVES 8

Vegetable oil, for brushing

2 ears **corn**, shucked (see Variation)

Nonstick cooking spray

½ cup **Mexican crema** or sour cream, at room temperature

5 tablespoons **salted butter**, melted

4 large **eggs**, at room temperature

2 **limes**

¼ cup **granulated sugar**

¼ cup **cornstarch**

1 teaspoon **garlic powder**

¼ teaspoon **ground cumin**

2 (14.75-ounce) cans **cream-style corn**

1 cup plus 2 tablespoons grated **Cotija cheese** or queso fresco, divided

1 teaspoon **Tajín chile-lime seasoning** or chili powder

Chopped **fresh cilantro**, for serving

1. Brush the grates of your grill with the oil, then heat to high (or oil a grill pan and heat over high heat). Add the corn directly to the grill and cook until just lightly charred on all sides, 8 to 10 minutes. Transfer to a cutting board, let cool for about 10 minutes, then use a sharp chef's knife to cut the kernels off the cobs. Slide 'em to the side, boos.

2. Position a rack in the center of the oven and preheat to 400°F. Liberally spray a 9-inch square (if you want the pudding thicker) or 9 by 13-inch (if you want it thinner) casserole dish with cooking spray.

3. In a large bowl, whisk together the crema, butter, and eggs until combined. Finely zest the limes and add the zest to the crema mixture (set the zested limes aside for serving). Add the sugar, cornstarch, garlic powder, and cumin, then stir in the grilled corn kernels and canned corn and mix until everything is well combined.

4. Pour the mixture into the prepared casserole dish and sprinkle with 1 cup of the Cotija cheese. Cover with aluminum foil and bake for 50 minutes, or until thickened to the consistency of pudding.

CELEBRATE!
Cinco de Mayo;
Memorial Day
barbecue; new
experiences

5. Remove from the oven. Sprinkle the pudding with the Tajín and the remaining 2 tablespoons Cotija and let sit for about 10 minutes. Cut the zested limes into wedges or slices, garnish the pudding with the cilantro, and serve it up hot, with the lime wedges on the top.

VARIATION

If corn is out of season or it's too cold to grill, you can use 1½ cups frozen corn, defrosted and patted dry. Instead of grilling the corn, cook it on the stovetop: In a large nonstick skillet, heat the oil over medium heat until shimmering. Add the corn in a single layer and cook, without stirring, until the kernels sizzle and pop and start to caramelize, 3 to 4 minutes. Toss the kernels well—they will have browned in spots—and spread them out in a single layer again. Cook until the kernels are browned all over, about 3 minutes more. Remove from the heat and let cool slightly before proceeding with the recipe. Some grocery stores (like Trader Joe's) also sell frozen charred corn, which allows you to bypass the caramelizing process.

Racism and discrimination ain't never been my bag; I've always been of the mindset that we're all mixed with a lil' bit of everything. After taking a DNA test a few years back, I learned that on top of my obvious African lineage, the bulk of it coming from Mali and Cameroon, I'm a little Irish with a sprinkle of Native American, East Asian, and Russian. And while some of us have the privilege to just prioritize equality on MLK Day or after the horrific shooting of an unarmed Black man by the police, the reality remains that we are all the same, even though civil rights are still a massive work in progress. Realizing that cultural marginalization was the inspo for this gratin, where Yukon Golds mingle with sweet potatoes, may feel heavy, but it's the truth. Each potato brings its own unique qualities into perfect harmony in this dish.

mixed-up potato gratin

SERVES 6 TO 8

1 pound **Yukon Gold potatoes**, peeled and sliced ⅛ inch thick

1 pound **sweet potatoes**, peeled and sliced ⅛ inch thick

2 teaspoons chopped **fresh thyme**

1 teaspoon chopped **fresh rosemary**

¾ teaspoon **kosher salt**

¾ teaspoon **freshly ground black pepper**

¾ teaspoon **smoked paprika**

¾ teaspoon **onion powder**

¾ teaspoon **garlic powder**

¼ teaspoon **cayenne pepper**

⅛ teaspoon **mustard powder**

⅛ teaspoon **freshly grated nutmeg**

3 tablespoons **unsalted butter**, plus more for greasing the pan

3 tablespoons **all-purpose flour**

1½ cups **half-and-half**

¼ cup **mascarpone cheese**, at room temperature

1 cup shredded **Gruyère cheese**, divided

1 cup shredded **Colby Jack cheese**, divided

Chopped **fresh parsley** or chives, for serving

1. In a large bowl filled with lukewarm water, rinse the potato slices. Line a large rimmed baking sheet with paper towels or clean kitchen towels and lay the potato slices over the towels in a single layer (you may need to layer more towels on top of the first layer of potatoes to fit them all). Thoroughly pat the slices dry with more kitchen or paper towels; set aside.

2. In a small bowl, whisk together the thyme, rosemary, salt, black pepper, paprika, onion powder, garlic powder, cayenne, mustard powder, and nutmeg until combined.

3. Position a rack in the middle of the oven and preheat to 400°F.

recipe continues

4. In a medium pot, melt the butter over medium heat. Whisk in the flour to form a roux and cook, stirring continuously, for 1 to 2 minutes. Whisk in the half-and-half, mascarpone, and half of the shredded cheeses, then whisk until the cheeses have melted into cheesy deliciousness and the sauce thickens slightly. Remove from the heat and set aside; the sauce may thicken as it sits—that's all good.

5. Liberally grease a 10-inch cast-iron skillet with butter. Transfer the potato slices to a large bowl, sprinkle with the seasoning mixture, and toss to evenly coat all the slices. Arrange the potato slices in the greased skillet, alternating 2 slices of Yukon Gold with 2 slices of sweet potato in a tight round circle closing into the center of the pan. Continue layering the potatoes until you run out. If you have any remaining slices of one type of potato and not the other, tuck 'em wherever you prefer, or just layer them on top.

6. Pour the cheese sauce over the potatoes and spread it out to the edges of the skillet with a small offset spatula. Sprinkle with the remaining shredded cheese. Cover the skillet with aluminum foil and bake for 50 minutes, then remove the foil and bake for 25 minutes more, or until the cheese is melted, bubbling, and golden.

7. Remove from the oven and let cool for 10 to 15 minutes (hard, I know!). Garnish with the parsley and serve it up.

CELEBRATE!
Martin Luther King Jr. Day; any heritage-month celebration; a friend of a different culture

Dressing is what we in the South call Northern stuffing. To be called the latter, it must go *inside* the turkey—if it's baked on its own, it ain't stuffing, boos. This cornbread dressing, layered with chicken meat, is one of my favorite recipes from Auntie Rose (the Queen of Dressing in the fam), who always makes twice the needed amount. She serves one pan at the holiday table and freezes the other or shares the extra with family and friends if she's feeling generous. I've halved her recipe below, but feel free to double it.

rose's cornbread dressing

SERVES 8 TO 10

CHICKEN AND CHICKEN STOCK

1 (3-pound) **whole chicken**, neck and giblets removed

4 **chicken bouillon cubes**

1 large **celery stalk**, quartered

1 medium **sweet onion**, quartered

6 tablespoons (¾ stick) **salted butter**

2 teaspoons **freshly ground black pepper**

1½ teaspoons minced or finely grated **garlic**

CORNBREAD

2½ cups (338 grams) **self-rising cornmeal**, such as Aunt Jemima Self-Rising Yellow Corn Meal Mix (see Note)

2½ tablespoons **all-purpose flour**

2½ teaspoons **granulated sugar**

1¼ cups **whole milk**, at room temperature

3 large **eggs**, at room temperature, beaten

½ cup (113 grams) **sour cream**, at room temperature

½ cup (1 stick/113 grams) **salted butter**, melted

2½ tablespoons **vegetable oil**

CORNBREAD DRESSING

1 medium **sweet onion**, finely chopped (about 1 cup)

1 large **celery stalk**, finely chopped (about 1 cup)

¼ cup finely chopped **green bell pepper**

½ (12-ounce) bag **herb-seasoned stuffing**, such as Pepperidge Farm

1 (10.5-ounce) can **cream of mushroom soup**

1 (10.5-ounce) can **cream of chicken soup**

4 **white sandwich bread slices** (include 1 heel)

1½ teaspoons **ground sage**

1½ teaspoons **poultry seasoning**

¾ teaspoon **freshly ground black pepper**

1. Make the chicken and chicken stock: Place the chicken breast-side down in an 8-quart pot and cover with 8 to 10 cups water, or enough to fully submerged the chicken.

2. Add the bouillion cubes, celery, onion, butter, black pepper, and garlic. Bring to a boil over high heat, then reduce the heat to medium-low. Skim any gray scum that appears

recipe continues

CELEBRATE!
Thanksgiving;
baptism; a friend
needing nourishment
and comfort after
having a baby

on the surface, cover, and cook, stirring occasionally to prevent the ingredients from sticking to the sides and bottom of the pot, until the breast meat is tender and can be easily pulled apart with a fork, 1 hour 30 minutes to 1 hour 45 minutes. Remove from the heat, uncover, and let cool for 1 hour, then cover the pot and pop it in the fridge overnight.

3. The following day, return the pot to low heat and warm it to room temperature. Remove the chicken from the pot and discard the skin, cartilage, and bones, leaving just the meat. Pull apart the meat and set it aside in a bowl. To keep the chicken from drying out, add a few tablespoons of the stock from the pot and stir to combine. Strain the remaining stock, pressing on the solids to extract as much liquid as possible, and set aside; discard the vegetables.

4. Make the cornbread: Position a rack in the middle of the oven and preheat to 375°F.

5. In a large bowl, whisk together the cornmeal, flour, and sugar until combined. In a medium bowl, whisk together the milk and eggs until combined. Add the wet ingredients to the dry ingredients and whisk to combine. Whisk in the sour cream until combined, followed by the melted butter. The batter will be slightly runny.

6. Heat a 9-inch cast-iron skillet over high heat until it's scorching hot. To test, add a few droplets of water; if they dance in the skillet, it's hot enough. Add the oil to the skillet and remove the pan from the heat. Pour the batter into the skillet—the oil will sizzle and bubble—and transfer to the oven. Bake for 35 to 45 minutes, until the cornbread is golden brown and a toothpick inserted into the center comes out mostly clean—you don't want to overbake. No dry cornbread round these parts. Transfer the skillet to a wire rack and let cool for about 20 minutes, then turn the cornbread out onto the rack and let cool to room temperature.

7. Make the cornbread dressing: Preheat the oven to 350°F.

8. Crumble the cornbread into a large bowl, breaking it up into super-small pieces and fine crumbs. Add the onion, celery, and bell pepper and, using your hands (disposable food gloves help here, y'all), add the stuffing mix to the bowl and mix until thoroughly combined.

9. Add the cream of mushroom and chicken soups and 3 cups of the homemade stock and stir until thoroughly combined. Make sure you are mixing as diligently as possible, so the flavor shines throughout.

10. Place the bread slices over the dressing mixture and pour 1 cup of the stock over the bread and dressing, soaking the bread, then mix thoroughly to incorporate the bread into the dressing mixture, breaking it up into smaller and smaller pieces until fully incorporated.

11. Season with the ground sage, poultry seasoning, and pepper and thoroughly mix to combine.

12. Spread a third of the dressing mixture on the bottom of a 9 by 13-inch pan. Top with half the shredded chicken and repeat with another third of the dressing and the remaining chicken. Finish with the remaining dressing.

13. Cover the pan with aluminum foil and bake for 45 minutes. (Sneak a peek midway through baking; should you notice the dressing starting to get dry, add a little extra stock to the top, then cover again.) Remove the foil and bake for 25 to 30 minutes more, until the dressing registers 180°F on an instant-read thermometer.

note If you can't find self-rising cornmeal, it's easy to make it yourself. For every 1 cup self-rising cornmeal, whisk together ¾ cup fine cornmeal, 3 tablespoons all-purpose flour, 1 tablespoon baking powder, and ½ teaspoon fine sea salt.

I'm a risk-taker by nature, but there've been many moments where a leap of faith felt like a life-and-death decision. It takes a lot of confidence and fortitude to stand at the fork in the road of your life and not waver on which path to take. Quitting my job to go all in for *Grandbaby Cakes* was terrifying. I didn't take the standard advice to have six months' salary tucked away and no debt—in fact, I had plenty of debt and next to no savings! But I just needed to take a leap regardless of whether it paid off—and in the beginning, it didn't. I had plenty of setbacks, but my grind was next-level.

Looking back, I wish I had rewarded myself more as my success climbed. So my wish for you is that you pause where you are now and celebrate. Take stock of the risks you've taken regardless of the payoff. This dish is a nice way to enjoy even the smallest successes. It highlights veggies and fruits in a dessert kinda way. Sweet, syrupy, full of flavor, and so damn good.

roasted mango, sweet potato, and butternut squash

SERVES 4

CELEBRATE!
Dinner partay;
Risk-and-Reward
Day (yep, I made
that up)

2 ripe **mangoes**, chopped into ½- to ¾-inch chunks (about 2 cups)

1 large **sweet potato**, peeled and chopped into ½- to ¾-inch chunks (about 2 cups)

10½ ounces **butternut squash**, peeled and chopped into ½- to ¾-inch chunks (about 2 cups)

½ cup (1 stick) **unsalted butter**, melted

¼ cup **maple syrup**

3 **garlic cloves**, minced or finely grated

1½ teaspoons **vanilla extract**

1 teaspoon **ground cinnamon**

½ teaspoon **smoked paprika**

¼ teaspoon **freshly grated nutmeg**

Pinch of **cayenne pepper**

2 teaspoons **kosher salt**

½ teaspoon **freshly ground black pepper**

Chopped **fresh cilantro**, for serving

1. Position a rack in the middle of the oven and preheat to 425°F. Line a 9 by 13-inch baking pan with parchment paper.

2. In a large bowl, toss the mango, sweet potato, and squash until combined. Transfer to the prepared baking pan and bake for 10 minutes, or until softened.

3. Meanwhile, in a medium bowl, whisk together the butter, maple syrup, garlic, vanilla, cinnamon, paprika, nutmeg, and cayenne until combined.

4. Remove the baking pan from the oven, drizzle with the butter mixture, and toss to make sure the ingredients are evenly coated. Season with salt and black pepper, then return the pan to the oven and bake, stirring every

5 to 10 minutes to prevent the syrup from burning, for 25 to 30 minutes more, until the syrup is caramelized and somewhat reduced and the mango, squash, and potato are completely tender.

5. Remove from the oven and transfer to a serving dish. Garnish with the cilantro and serve.

I spent my childhood avoiding Brussels sprouts, so the first time I gave them a try I was in my mid-twenties at a steak house in Las Vegas. When my friend Tisa ordered them for the table, the Brussels arrived crispy and irresistible, glazed with balsamic vinegar and honey. I ate two big helpings and nearly forgot about the sizzling filet sitting in front of me. Now Brussels sprouts remind me to try something new on the menu or in life.

duck fat brussels sprouts and pears

SERVES 6

CELEBRATE!
Getting your act together; closing a major bizness deal (you did it!)

⅓ cup **grapeseed oil** or other neutral oil

2 tablespoons **crushed red pepper flakes**

3 tablespoons **duck fat**

1 **shallot**, finely chopped

1 teaspoon minced or finely grated **garlic**

1 pound **Brussels sprouts**, trimmed and halved

1½ teaspoons **kosher salt**

1 **red pear**, halved, cored, and diced

1 teaspoon **freshly ground black pepper**

⅓ cup **maple syrup**

2 tablespoons **balsamic vinegar**

1 tablespoon **sriracha**

Finely grated **zest** of 1 **orange**

1 tablespoon **fresh orange juice**

½ cup **dried cranberries**

2 tablespoons chopped **fresh cilantro**, for serving (optional)

1. In a small pot, bring the oil and red pepper flakes to a gentle simmer over medium-low heat. Let the oil infuse until it turns slightly red, about 5 minutes. Strain through a fine-mesh sieve into a small bowl and set aside; discard the red pepper flakes.

2. In a large cast-iron skillet, melt the duck fat over medium heat. Add the shallot and cook, stirring, until coated in the fat, about 1 minute. Stir in the garlic and cook until aromatic, about 30 seconds.

3. Toss in the Brussels sprouts, season with the salt, and cook, stirring, until the Brussels sprouts start to soften, about 7 minutes. Add

the pear and black pepper and cook, stirring, until the pear starts to soften, 4 to 5 minutes. Raise the heat to medium-high and add the maple syrup, vinegar, sriracha, orange zest, and orange juice. Cook, stirring from time to time, until everything is evenly coated and the liquid reduces slightly, 3 to 4 minutes. The Brussels sprouts should be tender. (If you prefer them more crisp-tender, cook them for 3 to 4 minutes before adding the pears.)

4. Drizzle in the chile oil—start with a little at first, then taste and add more, or all of it, if you like—add the cranberries, and toss gently to combine. Garnish with the cilantro, if desired, and serve.

I remember helping Big Mama wash collards in the sink of her Mississippi kitchen. We scrubbed them until they were pearly green—grit and dirt didn't stand a chance. Then came the laid-back braise to develop their silky, delicate texture and smoky, meaty, fall-off-the-bone counterpart. After a couple of hours, a nourishing and flavorful pot likker was ready for sopping up with cornbread (page 115). My mama changed up Big Mama's recipe by adding apple cider vinegar, bouillon, and red pepper flakes to deepen the collards' flavor and add a hint more heat, and she even updated the ham hock, swapping it out for smoked turkey to please the non-pork-eaters. I'm so glad she shared her version with me so I can pass it to you. If you like, mix up your collards with mustard greens.

mama's collards

SERVES 8 TO 10

CELEBRATE!
The ultimate
Sunday supper
(one does not exist
without greens)

3 pounds **collard greens** (5 or 6 smaller bunches), leaves stemmed

1 to 1½ pounds **smoked turkey wings**, legs, or necks, or ham hock (make sure they're meaty)

2 teaspoons **chicken bouillon**, such as Better Than Bouillon

2 slices **turkey bacon** or pork bacon, coarsely chopped

½ cup finely chopped **yellow onion**

3 tablespoons packed **dark brown sugar**

1 tablespoon **apple cider vinegar**, plus more (optional) for serving

2 teaspoons **seasoned salt**, such as Lawry's

2 teaspoons **Worcestershire sauce**

1 teaspoon **crushed red pepper flakes**

½ teaspoon **garlic powder**

½ teaspoon **smoked paprika**

Cornbread (like my Honeychile Brown Butter Cornbread, page 115), for serving

Hot sauce and/or pepper sauce, for serving

1. Take a handful of greens and stack them on top of one another, then roll them up tightly lengthwise like a cigar. Slice the roll crosswise into ½-inch-thick strips. Repeat with the remaining leaves.

2. Transfer the greens to a clean sink filled with cold water and swoosh them around to remove dirt, sand, and debris. Drain and repeat until the water is clear and the greens are grit-free. Leave them in the cold water until ready to use.

3. In a large soup pot, combine the smoked turkey with enough water to fully submerge the meat, 10 cups or more. Stir in the bouillon. Bring to a boil over medium-high heat, then reduce the heat to low, cover, and cook at a gentle simmer until the smoked meat is nearly tender, about 45 minutes. To test this, stick a fork in the center of the meat and twist; it should flake if ready.

4. Once the turkey is almost tender, add an additional 4 cups water, the bacon, onion, brown sugar, vinegar, seasoned salt, Worcestershire, red pepper flakes, garlic powder, and paprika and stir to combine. Drain the greens, shaking off excess water, and add them to the pot.

5. Raise the heat to medium-high and bring to a boil. Reduce the heat to medium-low, partially cover the pot so the steam can escape, and cook until the greens are silky and tender, the meat is falling off the bone, and much of the water has evaporated, leaving a concentrated,

flavorful broth that barely covers the greens (this is your pot likker, y'all). (If you have more water than that, keeping cooking it down.) Taste the pot likker: It should taste restorative and have deep smoky and umami notes.

6. Serve with cornbread and hot sauce, if desired.

note To pick wonderful greens at your local grocery store or farmers' market, pay close attention to the leaves. They shouldn't be too tough and should be easy to pull away from the stem and tear or cut later when you're prepping them to cook.

Don't just feed your body.
Feed your soul. —*jocelyn*

legumes, grains & vegetable mains

I always aspired to be more of a runner—I tried once before with a couch-to-5k program, but got bored, no matter how much Beyoncé I listened to. When my coauthor, Olga, encouraged me to start again, I approached running differently: Older and wiser, I told myself quitting wasn't an option. Each week since that day (what I call my "Rocky moment"), I've run three times a week, rain or shine.

After an intense workout, you need a nutrient-dense meal, and these power bowls, made with black-eyed peas, sweet potatoes, and avocado, are ideal not only for fueling your body but also for celebrating your own Rocky moment. I plan to enjoy these when I run my very first marathon, and I know I won't quit this time.

black-eyed pea power bowls

SERVES 4

SWEET POTATOES
1 large **sweet potato**, peeled and cubed (about 1 pound)
1 tablespoon **extra-virgin olive oil**
¾ teaspoon **kosher salt**
½ teaspoon **ground cumin**
½ teaspoon **smoked paprika**
⅛ teaspoon **cayenne pepper**

BLACK-EYED PEAS
1 (15-ounce) can **black-eyed peas**, drained and rinsed
¼ cup **chicken stock**, vegetable stock, or water
2 **garlic cloves**, minced or finely grated
2 teaspoons **fresh lime juice**
1 canned **chipotle pepper in adobo sauce**, finely chopped
1 teaspoon **ground cumin**
½ teaspoon **kosher salt**

CURRIED GREEN GODDESS DRESSING
1 cup **plain full-fat Greek yogurt** or vegan Greek yogurt
⅓ cup loosely packed **fresh cilantro**
⅓ cup loosely packed **fresh basil**
⅓ cup loosely packed **fresh flat-leaf parsley**
2 **garlic cloves**
1 tablespoon **fresh lime juice**
2 teaspoons **curry powder**
¾ teaspoon **kosher salt**
⅛ teaspoon **cayenne pepper**

TO SERVE
Cooked grain of your choice, such as brown rice, quinoa, farro, or cauliflower rice
Pickled Onion (see page 90) or sliced red onion
2 ripe **avocados**, halved, pitted, and sliced
Fresh cilantro leaves, for serving

recipe continues

1. **Roast the sweet potato:** Position a rack in the middle of the oven and preheat to 400°F.

2. In a medium bowl, toss together the sweet potato, olive oil, salt, cumin, paprika, and cayenne. Transfer to a large rimmed baking sheet and roast for 20 minutes. Toss it up, then roast for another 20 minutes, or until the potato is nicely browned and tender.

3. **Make the black-eyed peas:** While the sweet potato is roasting, in a small pot, combine the black-eyed peas, stock, garlic, lime juice, chipotle, cumin, and salt and bring to a boil over medium heat. Reduce the heat to low and simmer until the flavors have melded, about 5 minutes. Remove from the heat, cover, and set aside.

4. **Make the Green Goddess dressing:** In a blender, combine the yogurt, cilantro, basil, parsley, garlic, lime juice, curry powder, salt, and cayenne and blend until smooth. Transfer to a 12-ounce jar and slide to the side.

5. When ready to assemble, divide the grain of your choice, peas, and sweet potato among four bowls. Top with pickled onion, avocado, and a drizzle of the dressing. Garnish with the cilantro and serve it up. Refrigerate the leftovers in an airtight container for up to 7 days for fast meal assembly on the go (bomb meal prep option!).

CELEBRATE!
Your first 5k;
exercising for a full
week; getting up
without hitting the
snooze button

I'm a hard-core meat lover—give me fried chicken or steak any day—but during the COVID-19 pandemic, I began eating mostly vegetarian and vegan on weekdays. It started when my friends Meiko and Kenneth decided they would eat vegan five days a week and then go absolutely HAM on whatever they wanted to eat on weekends. I loved their approach and decided to give it a try. I found it surprisingly easier than I had thought it would be. It brought me so much joy to experiment with recipes and find even better replacements for some of my favorite meaty dishes. Sometimes my zany ideas worked and other times not so much. Lentils ended up being a must-have. When I made these meatballs for the first time, I created variations such as meatballs and spaghetti and Mediterranean-inflected meals, but this piccata stew with orzo became the champ among them all. Giving all the classic Italian vibes with a bomb remix, each bite of this stew provides the ultimate tranquility and joy.

lentil meatball piccata stew with orzo

SERVES 4 TO 6

LENTIL MEATBALLS

3 tablespoons **extra-virgin olive oil**, divided

5 **white button mushroom caps**, chopped

¼ cup chopped **white onion**

1 **garlic clove**, minced or finely grated

2 (15-ounce) cans **lentils**, drained and rinsed

½ cup **plain bread crumbs**

1½ teaspoons **Worcestershire sauce** (see Note)

1 teaspoon **Italian Seasoning** (page 64) or store-bought

½ teaspoon **kosher salt**

¼ teaspoon **freshly ground black pepper**

¼ teaspoon **crushed red pepper flakes**

1 large **egg** or egg replacer equivalent

STEW

1 tablespoon **extra-virgin olive oil**

1 tablespoon **unsalted butter**

3 medium **carrots**, finely chopped (see Note)

2 **celery stalks**, finely chopped (see Note)

½ large **white onion**, finely diced (see Note)

1½ teaspoons **kosher salt**, plus more to taste

½ teaspoon **freshly ground black pepper**, plus more to taste

4 **garlic cloves**, minced or finely grated

2 tablespoons **all-purpose flour**

4 cups **vegetable stock**, divided

1 cup **dry white wine**

Finely grated **zest and juice** of 1 **lemon**

½ teaspoon **Italian Seasoning** (page 64) or store-bought

1 sprig **rosemary**

¼ teaspoon **crushed red pepper flakes** (optional)

1 **bay leaf**

1 cup **uncooked orzo**

2 tablespoons drained **capers**

Chopped **fresh flat-leaf parsley**, for serving

Lemon wedges, for serving

recipe continues

CELEBRATE!
Meatless Mondays;
first day of fall;
a vegan dinner party;
Earth Day

1. **Make the lentil meatballs:** In a medium nonstick skillet, heat 1 tablespoon of the olive oil over medium heat until shimmering. Add the mushrooms and onion and cook, stirring, until softened and the onion turns translucent, about 6 minutes. Stir in the garlic and cook until aromatic, about 30 seconds, then remove from the heat and transfer to a food processor.

2. Add the lentils to the food processor and pulse until the mixture is well blended and the lentils have mostly broken down but are not yet mushy, 8 to 10 pulses.

3. Transfer the lentil mixture to a large bowl, then throw in the bread crumbs, Worcestershire, Italian seasoning, salt, black pepper, and red pepper flakes and mix until well combined. Add the egg and mix to incorporate. Form the mixture into balls, using a little less than ¼ cup for each one (you may need to dampen your palms if the mixture is too sticky). You should get 12 meatballs. (If you want your meatballs to better maintain their shape during cooking, refrigerate for 30 minutes before moving on.)

4. In the skillet you used for the mushrooms, heat 1 tablespoon of the olive oil over medium heat until shimmering. Line a large plate with paper towels and set it near your work area. Add half the meatballs to the pan and cook until brown all over, about 12 minutes total. Transfer the cooked meatballs to the prepared plate and repeat with the remaining 1 tablespoon olive oil and meatballs.

5. **Make the stew:** In a large soup pot, heat the oil and butter over medium-high heat until the butter melts. Add the carrots, celery, and onion, season with the salt and black pepper, and cook, stirring, until tender, about 5 minutes. Stir in the garlic and cook until aromatic, about 30 seconds, then stir in the flour and cook for 1 to 2 minutes. Pour in 1 cup of the stock and cook until the flour has completely dissolved into the liquid, about 1 minute—this will ensure the raw flour taste is cooked out.

6. Add the remaining 3 cups stock, the wine, lemon zest, lemon juice, Italian seasoning, rosemary, red pepper flakes (if using), and bay leaf and season with salt and pepper to taste. Stir in 1 cup water and bring the soup to a boil, then stir in the orzo. Reduce the heat to maintain a simmer, cover, and cook until the orzo is cooked through, about 15 minutes.

7. Add the capers, taste, and season with additional salt and/or black pepper, if desired. Add the lentil meatballs to the pot and stir to combine. Cook until the meatballs are heated through, about 5 minutes. Discard the bay leaf. Ladle the stew into bowls, garnish with parsley, and serve hot with the lemon wedges for squeezing.

notes To save time, you can quarter the carrots, celery, and onion and pulse them in a food processor, one vegetable at a time, until finely chopped. You'll use the food processor for processing the lentil mixture, too, so don't bother washing between the uses. Ain't nobody got time for that!

If you want to keep the dish vegan, use an egg replacer and seek out vegan Worcestershire sauce, such as Annie's brand, my jam.

About ten years ago, I started obsessing over my purpose: I had previously thought it was tied to a profession or a "thing" and at first believed my purpose was *Grandbaby Cakes*. But once my daughter, Harmony, was born, I thought it was her. Soon I realized that one's purpose was not fixed but changed with time. The Pixar movie *Soul* sums this up beautifully: At the end of the day, one's purpose is to just be and live. And with this epiphany, I found the peace that comes when you know that waking up and being present in your life is precisely what matters.

Take these tacos: Their only real mission is to be delicious and provide joy with each bite. It don't have to be that deep, y'all.

mango jerk jackfruit tacos

SERVES 4

JERK JACKFRUIT
1 large **white onion**, coarsely chopped
4 **scallions**, chopped into large pieces
4 **garlic cloves**
1 to 2 **Scotch bonnet chiles**, seeded (see Note)
Leaves from 8 sprigs **thyme**
½ cup **mango nectar**
¼ cup packed **dark brown sugar**
3 tablespoons **grapeseed oil**
3 tablespoons **soy sauce** or tamari
2 tablespoons **apple cider vinegar**

1 tablespoon **kosher salt**
2 teaspoons **ground allspice**
2 teaspoons grated **fresh ginger**
1 teaspoon **ground cinnamon**
½ teaspoon **freshly grated nutmeg**
½ teaspoon **freshly ground black pepper**
2 (14-ounce) cans **jackfruit in brine**

MANGO SALSA
2 cups finely diced **mango** (from 1 to 2 mangoes)

⅓ cup chopped **fresh cilantro leaves**
¼ cup diced **fresh tomatoes**
½ **red bell pepper**, seeded and finely diced
½ medium **red onion**, finely diced
1 small **jalapeño**, seeded and finely diced
2 tablespoons **fresh lime juice**, or to taste
Kosher salt

12 **corn tortillas**, warmed in a lightly greased skillet, for serving

1. Marinate the jackfruit: In a blender, combine the white onion, scallions, garlic, chiles, thyme, mango nectar, brown sugar, oil, soy sauce, vinegar, salt, allspice, ginger, cinnamon, nutmeg, and black pepper and blend until smooth.

2. Drain the jackfruit and transfer to a large bowl. Using your fingers or two forks, shred the jackfruit chunks as you would for pulled pork or chicken. Add the jerk sauce, cover, and refrigerate for at least 2 and up to 8 hours.

CELEBRATE!
Taco Tuesday;
Caribbean night;
an exciting meal
the night before
vacay

3. **Make the mango salsa:** Shortly before you're ready to cook and serve the tacos, in a medium bowl, stir together the mango, cilantro, tomatoes, bell pepper, red onion, jalapeño, and lime juice until combined. Season to taste with salt and let it chill-mode for 10 minutes.

4. **Make the tacos:** When ready to cook, transfer the jackfruit with the jerk sauce to a large skillet and heat over medium heat, stirring occasionally, until warmed through, 5 to 7 minutes. Spoon the jackfruit over the warmed tortillas, top with the salsa, and get ready for a flavor bomb, boos!

note You can use 2 tablespoons Scotch bonnet hot sauce as a swap for the fresh Scotch bonnets.

CELEBRATE!
Mardi Gras; first
day of fall (or when
the weather has that
crisp chill); Meatless
Monday

Beans were a staple for me growing up. My mother would cook all the beans: pinto, lima, butter beans. Since she was a working mom, she'd throw them in the Crockpot in the morning, and come dinnertime, there were brothy, creamy beans for us to eat. To infuse the beans with even more flavor, my mom would throw in a ham hock or smoked turkey wing. When my brother became vegan, it inspired me to reimagine my favorite childhood recipes. And when I discovered vegan chorizo—baby, bye!—I immediately tried using it here. My mother, the queen of the turkey leg and ham hock, loved it, too, and couldn't even believe it was vegan!

vegan red beans and rice

SERVES 8

2 tablespoons **extra-virgin olive oil**

1 small **yellow onion**, finely chopped (about 1 cup)

1 large **celery stalk**, finely chopped (about ½ cup)

½ **green bell pepper**, finely chopped (about ½ cup)

8 ounces **soy chorizo**, such as Frieda's Soyrizo or No Evil El Capitán, casings removed, if it's in casings

1 tablespoon minced or finely grated **garlic**

2 or 3 **vegetable bouillon cubes**

2 tablespoons **hot sauce**

1 tablespoon **vegan Worcestershire sauce**, such as Annie's

1½ to 2 teaspoons **No-Salt Cajun Seasoning** (page 37) or store-bought

1 teaspoon **kosher salt**, or more to taste

¼ to ½ teaspoon **cayenne pepper** (optional)

⅛ teaspoon **freshly ground black pepper**, or more to taste

1 pound **dried red beans**, picked over for debris, soaked overnight, and drained

Cooked rice, for serving

Chopped **fresh chives**, for serving (optional)

1. In a large heavy-bottomed pot, heat the olive oil over medium heat until shimmering. Add the onion, celery, and bell pepper and cook, stirring, until the vegetables begin to soften and caramelize, 8 to 10 minutes. Add the soy chorizo and cook, stirring, until browned, 4 to 5 minutes. Add the garlic and cook, stirring, until aromatic, about 1 minute—don't let the garlic burn.

2. Raise the heat to medium-high and stir in the bouillon cubes, hot sauce, Worcestershire, Cajun seasoning, salt, cayenne, and black pepper. Add 7 cups water, then stir in the beans. Raise the heat to high and bring the liquid to a boil. Reduce the heat to low, cover, and cook until the beans are tender, about 2 hours. Uncover and simmer the stew until the liquid thickens, about 30 minutes. Taste and season with more salt and black pepper, if desired, then remove from the heat. Let the beans and sauce stand until thickened slightly, about 15 minutes, then divide among bowls and serve with rice topped with chives (if using).

After I gave birth, I tried every diet to get snatched, but the one that worked for me was Paleo. During this phase, I relied on cauliflower, mashed and riced, to provide me with a semblance of the carb fix I craved. Eventually, I landed on something that felt more intuitive. The lesson I took away from Dietgate was relearning to love my body, which had changed considerably and wasn't snapping back like the celebs were showing (maybe because I didn't have a coterie of trainers, personal chefs, and stylists?). With time, I accepted what I perceived as my body's flaws and learned to treat them as strengths and to nourish and celebrate what I had. My body was strong and capable. I birthed a human. Still, sometimes low-carb versions of my favorite foods are what I crave, not to deprive my body, but instead to nourish it. This is a twist on one of my favorite Lowcountry dishes, red rice—now packed with veggies. Whether you want to eat low-carb or just love cauliflower, you can celebrate with this flavorful dish. I promise you won't miss the rice.

savannah red cauliflower rice

SERVES 6 TO 8

1 teaspoon **extra-virgin olive oil**

4 ounces **bacon**, diced

1 pound **smoked sausage**, such as andouille, sliced

1 large **yellow onion**, finely diced

1 **green bell pepper**, finely diced

1 **celery stalk**, finely diced

¼ teaspoon **kosher salt**

3¼ teaspoons **No-Salt Cajun Seasoning** (page 37) or store-bought, divided

4 **garlic cloves**, minced or finely grated

2 **bay leaves**

1 (14-ounce) can **diced tomatoes**, with their juices

1 (15-ounce) can **tomato sauce**

¾ cup **low-sodium chicken stock**

2 tablespoons **tomato paste**

2 teaspoons **hot sauce**

1 teaspoon **light brown sugar**

1 teaspoon **Worcestershire sauce**

½ teaspoon **cayenne pepper**

1 (12-ounce) bag **frozen cauliflower rice**

12 ounces large **shrimp**, peeled and deveined

¼ cup chopped **fresh flat-leaf parsley**, for serving

1. Position a rack in the middle of the oven and preheat to 350°F. Line a small baking sheet with paper towels.

2. In a large Dutch oven, heat the olive oil over medium-high heat until shimmering. Add the bacon and cook, stirring, until golden brown and starting to crisp up, about 5 minutes. Using a slotted spoon, transfer the bacon to the prepared baking sheet. Add the sausage to the pot and cook until browned, about 5 minutes, then transfer to a plate and set aside.

3. Add the onion, bell pepper, celery, salt, and ¼ teaspoon of the Cajun seasoning to the pot, then reduce the heat to medium and cook,

CELEBRATE!
A friend who just
had a baby; a Friday
meal at the end of a
crazy workweek

stirring, until softened, 5 to 6 minutes. Stir in the garlic and bay leaves and cook until aromatic, about 30 seconds. Stir in the sausage, half the cooked bacon, the diced tomatoes, tomato sauce, stock, tomato paste, 1 teaspoon of the Cajun seasoning, the hot sauce, brown sugar, Worcestershire, and cayenne until combined. Stir in the cauliflower rice, cover, and transfer to the oven. Bake for 30 minutes, or until everything is saucy and softened.

4. In a medium bowl, season the shrimp with the remaining 2 teaspoons Cajun seasoning and toss to coat. Add the shrimp and the remaining bacon to the Dutch oven, cover, and bake for 5 to 7 minutes, until the shrimp become pink and opaque. Remove from the oven, discard the bay leaves, sprinkle with the parsley, and serve.

CELEBRATE!
New Year's Day; any
time you feel
like you need a lil'
bit of luck

This Lowcountry staple of black-eyed peas, fatty meats, and rice was introduced to America by enslaved Africans. The dish, believed to bring good luck, is often served alongside collards (page 128), and the two are ubiquitous on New Year's Day and throughout the year. (The old-schoolers always added a dime to our New Year's batch of peas to symbolize acquiring wealth in the coming year.) When highlighting recipes with roots in the African diaspora, I start by honoring its past. My ancestors' creation of this dish gave me an opportunity to use warm curry spices and skip the meat but maintain the foundation of peas, okra, and rice.

vegan curry jumpin' john

SERVES 6 TO 8

2 tablespoons **extra-virgin olive oil**

1 medium **yellow onion**, finely chopped

1 **poblano pepper**, chopped

1 **celery stalk**, diced

4 **garlic cloves**, minced

2 teaspoons grated **fresh ginger**

6 ounces **okra**, stemmed and cut into 1-inch pieces

1 (12-ounce) bag **frozen black-eyed peas**

2 cups **vegetable stock**

1 (13.5-ounce) can **full-fat coconut milk**

2 tablespoons **curry powder**

2 teaspoons **kosher salt**, or more to taste

1 teaspoon **ground cumin**

1 teaspoon **No-Salt Cajun Seasoning** (page 37) or store-bought

1 teaspoon **freshly ground black pepper**, or more to taste

¼ teaspoon **ground cinnamon**

¼ teaspoon **cayenne pepper**

1 cup **basmati rice**

Chopped **fresh flat-leaf parsley**, for garnish

Hot sauce, for serving

1. In a large pot, heat the olive oil over medium heat until shimmering. Add the onion, poblano, and celery and cook, stirring, until the onion is becoming translucent, 4 to 5 minutes. Add the garlic and ginger and cook until aromatic, about 30 seconds. Stir in the okra and cook for another 30 seconds.

2. Add the black-eyed peas, stock, coconut milk, curry powder, salt, cumin, Cajun seasoning, black pepper, cinnamon, and cayenne. Raise the heat to medium-high and

bring to a boil. Reduce the heat to medium-low and simmer, uncovered, until the peas become more tender, about 20 minutes.

3. Stir in the rice, reduce the heat to low, cover, and simmer until the black-eyed peas are tender and the rice is cooked through, 25 to 35 minutes. Fluff everything together. Taste and season with more salt and/or black pepper, if desired, then divide among bowls, garnish with the parsley, and serve, with hot sauce, of course.

Someone once told me that altering traditional foods was condescending and disrespectful. It was upsetting to hear, considering I built my career on doing just that: remixing classic recipes with a modern twist. After mulling over my approach, I felt even more committed to it. While I stay true to certain traditional recipes, innovation and reinterpretation can be a beautiful way to bridge the past and the present.

This recipe is my way of connecting traditional Southern dirty rice with a creamy, indulgent risotto, a mash-up of two classics. Some may call it blasphemy, but I call it damn delish.

dirty rice risotto

SERVES 6

CELEBRATE!
Speaking in public
for the first time;
sharing with a
newfound friend

1⅓ cups **Arborio rice**

2 cups **chicken stock**

2 **bay leaves**

1 pound **chicken gizzards**, cleaned

8 ounces **chicken livers**, trimmed

2½ teaspoons **No-Salt Cajun Seasoning** (page 37) or store-bought

1 teaspoon **garlic powder**

1 teaspoon minced **fresh thyme leaves**

¼ teaspoon **cayenne pepper**

4 tablespoons **duck fat** or extra-virgin olive oil, divided

1 pound **ground beef** (preferably 80/20)

1½ teaspoons **kosher salt**

1 teaspoon **freshly ground black pepper**

1 small **onion**, diced

½ **green bell pepper**, seeded and diced

½ **red bell pepper**, seeded and diced

½ cup diced **celery**

5 **garlic cloves**, minced or finely grated

⅓ cup **heavy cream**

3 tablespoons **unsalted butter**

2 tablespoons **Worcestershire sauce**

2 teaspoons **hot sauce**

1 bunch **scallions**, sliced, plus more for garnish

Fresh parsley, for garnish

1. In a large pot, combine the rice, stock, and bay leaves and bring to a boil over medium-high heat. Cover and reduce the heat to the lowest setting. Cook until the rice is somewhat tender and the liquid has mostly evaporated, 10 to 15 minutes. Remove from the heat, fluff with a fork, and set aside. Keep the rice covered while you cook the rest of the dish.

2. In a medium pot, bring 2 cups water to a boil over high heat. Add the gizzards and cook

until cooked through, about 10 minutes. Use a slotted spoon or spider to transfer the gizzards to a food processor (keep the water in the pot at a boil) and process until it resembles ground meat, about 30 seconds. Transfer to a bowl and slide to the side.

3. Add the livers to the pot of boiling water and cook until cooked through, about 5 minutes, then remove the pot from the heat. Using a slotted spoon or spider, transfer the livers to

the food processor and pulse until coarsely ground. Reserve the cooking liquid.

4. In a small bowl, whisk up the Cajun seasoning, garlic powder, thyme, and cayenne. In a large skillet, melt 2 tablespoons of the duck fat over medium-high heat, then heat until shimmering. Add the ground beef, season with the salt, black pepper, and 1 teaspoon of the seasoning mixture, and cook, stirring and breaking up the meat with a wooden spoon, until the meat is browned and cooked through, 8 to 10 minutes. Stir in the gizzards and livers and cook until warmed through, about 2 minutes, then transfer the meat to a large bowl.

5. Add the remaining 2 tablespoons duck fat to the skillet, followed by the onion, green and red bell peppers, and celery. Cook, stirring, until softened, 6 to 8 minutes. Stir in the garlic and cook until aromatic, about 30 seconds. Remove from the heat.

6. Add the beef mixture, the cooked veggies, and the remaining seasoning blend to the rice and stir until well combined. Stir in the cream, 1 cup of the reserved gizzard-liver cooking liquid, the butter, Worcestershire, hot sauce, and scallions and cook over low to medium-low heat, stirring, until the rice is voluptuous and has absorbed all the liquid. Remove from the heat, divide among six bowls, and serve it up.

You simply can't live an amazing life if the food on your plate ain't amazing, boos! —*jocelyn*

seafood

This recipe, which blends island flavors with a decadent seafood dish, is a nod to my love of travel. When I was little, my parents tried to show my brother and me as much of the world as possible. Travel teaches you to welcome experiences different from what you're used to. My parents took us to the Caribbean, where I fell in love with the vibrant, intense flavors of the food and the laid-back island vibe. This snapper, stuffed with richly seasoned crab and topped with a punchy ginger-lime sauce (these flavors ain't playin'), is a nod to the region. If you can't get to the Caribbean, let the Caribbean come to you.

caribbean crab-stuffed snapper with ginger-lime sauce
SERVES 4

CELEBRATE!
Island night in the backyard (drop that reggae playlist!); staycation dinner

CRAB-STUFFED SNAPPER
4 tablespoons (½ stick) **salted butter**, divided
1 tablespoon **extra-virgin olive oil**
8 ounces **jumbo lump crabmeat**
½ cup **plain bread crumbs**
1 medium **shallot**, finely chopped
2 **garlic cloves**, minced or finely grated
⅓ cup **mayonnaise**
2 tablespoons **hot sauce**
1 tablespoon chopped **fresh flat-leaf parsley**
3½ teaspoons **Jerk Seasoning** (page 77) or store-bought, divided
1 teaspoon **garlic powder**
1 teaspoon **Old Bay seasoning**
¼ teaspoon **ground cumin**
Juice of 1 **lime** (about 2 tablespoons)
2 (2-pound) **whole red snappers**

GINGER-LIME SAUCE
4 tablespoons (½ stick) **salted butter**, divided
1 tablespoon finely chopped **shallot**
1 **garlic clove**, minced or finely grated
3 tablespoons **dry white wine**
1½ tablespoons **fresh lime juice**
½ teaspoon **Jerk Seasoning** (page 77) or store-bought
¼ teaspoon grated **fresh ginger**

1. Make the crab-stuffed snapper: Position a rack in the middle of the oven and preheat to 400°F. Line a large rimmed baking sheet with parchment paper.

2. In a medium nonstick skillet, heat 1 tablespoon of the butter and the olive oil over medium-high heat until the butter has melted. Add the crabmeat, bread crumbs, shallot, and garlic and cook, stirring, until the bread crumbs are toasted and golden, 4 to 5 minutes. Remove from the heat and set aside.

3. In a medium bowl, whisk together the mayonnaise, hot sauce, parsley, 1½ teaspoons of the jerk seasoning, the garlic powder, Old Bay, cumin, and lime juice until thoroughly combined. Fold in the crab mixture until combined.

4. Place the fish on the prepared baking sheet and sprinkle on both sides with the remaining 2 teaspoons jerk seasoning. Divide the crab mixture evenly between the cavities of the two fish, then top each fish evenly with 1½ tablespoons of the remaining butter.

5. Bake for about 30 minutes, until the fish is opaque and flakes easily with a fork.

6. **Make the sauce:** While the fish is baking, in a saucepan, melt 1 tablespoon of the butter over medium heat. Add the shallot and garlic and cook, stirring often, until tender and fragrant, about 2 minutes. Add the wine, lime juice, jerk seasoning, and ginger and bring to a boil, then cook until slightly thickened, about 2 minutes. Turn off the heat and stir in the remaining 3 tablespoons butter until it completely melts into the sauce. Serve the snapper family-style, with the sauce on the side.

Throw some refined, classy lobster into a hot dog bun, and it brings the whole thing back down to Earth. And when it comes to your lobster roll preference, are you Team Mayo or Team Butter? I roll with butter, because butter is bae all day. I opt for a brioche bun and put my own twist on this classic by spiking a puddle of butter with my fave Cajun seasoning.

cajun lobster rolls
SERVES 6

6 tablespoons (¾ stick) **unsalted butter**, divided
1½ tablespoons **No-Salt Cajun Seasoning** (page 37) or store-bought
4 **garlic cloves**, minced or finely grated

¼ teaspoon **kosher salt**, plus more to taste
¼ cup chopped **fresh chives**
3 tablespoons chopped **fresh dill**
2 tablespoons chopped **fresh flat-leaf parsley**, plus more for garnish

Juice of ½ **lemon**
Chilled meat from 3 cooked **lobsters** (1¼ to 1½ pounds each), coarsely diced (3 to 3½ cups meat)
6 **brioche hot dog buns**
Lemon wedges, for serving

1. Position a rack in the middle of the oven and preheat to 450°F.

2. In a small microwave-safe bowl, melt 2 tablespoons of the butter in 15-second bursts. (Butter tends to explode all over your microwave, so short bursts are best. You've been warned!)

3. In a large skillet, melt the remaining 4 tablespoons butter over medium heat. Add the Cajun seasoning, garlic, and salt and cook, stirring continuously, until fragrant, then stir in the chives, dill, parsley, and lemon juice to incorporate. Add the lobster and cook, stirring, until warmed through, about 2 minutes. Taste and season with additional salt, if ya like. Remove from the heat and set aside.

4. Brush the melted butter on the inside of the buns and place them on a large rimmed baking sheet. Toast in the oven until the buns are golden, 2 to 3 minutes.

5. Divide the warm lobster among the toasted buns, garnish with the parsley, and serve it up with lemon wedges on the side for squeezing.

CELEBRATE!
Lobster is on sale; summer get-together; backyard date night, BYOBB (blanket and bubbly)

Every year for Thanksgiving we go to Winona, Mississippi. Recently we've started also dropping by New Orleans—just a few hours away from Winona—for the weekend. I love New Orleans's wealth of Cajun and Creole food. We catch the Bayou Classic game and spend a lot of time walking around and eating. And no trip is complete without shrimp étouffée. The thick roux-based gravy reminds me of traditional Southern cooking, where smothering is a popular way to prepare protein. At some point, I realized that shrimp étouffée begs to be tucked into a potpie. It might not be traditional, but a flaky, buttery crust over spicy, saucy shrimp is a comfort meal you didn't know you needed.

CELEBRATE! An HBCU or other big football game; first-date anniversary; getting your driver's license!

shrimp étouffée potpie

SERVES 4 OR 5

4 tablespoons (½ stick) **salted butter**

6 tablespoons **all-purpose flour**, plus more as needed

½ large **yellow onion**, chopped

2 **celery stalks**, sliced

1 medium **green bell pepper**, chopped

4 teaspoons **No-Salt Cajun Seasoning** (page 37) or store-bought, divided

2 teaspoons **kosher salt**, divided

3 **garlic cloves**, minced or finely grated

1 **bay leaf**

2½ cups **chicken stock**

1 tablespoon **Worcestershire sauce**

1 pound medium **shrimp**, peeled and deveined

¼ cup chopped **scallions**, plus more for garnish

1 teaspoon **freshly ground black pepper**

1 (14-ounce) roll **puff pastry**, such as Dufour brand (all butta, baby!), defrosted in the refrigerator overnight

2 tablespoons **heavy cream**

1 large **egg**

1. Position a rack in the middle of the oven and preheat to 400°F.

2. Heat an ovenproof 9-inch skillet over medium heat for 1 minute. Add the butter and let it melt, then cook until the butter is browned and bubbling. Whisk in the flour, ensuring there are no lumps, then cook, stirring frequently, until the roux turns peanut butter brown, being careful to not burn it, 2 to 3 minutes.

3. Add the onion, celery, bell pepper, 2 teaspoons of the Cajun seasoning, and 1 teaspoon of the salt and cook, stirring frequently, until the onion is translucent, about 3 minutes. Add the garlic and bay leaf and cook, stirring, until fragrant, about 30 seconds. Add the stock in three additions, whisking to incorporate and ensuring there are no lumps after each addition.

4. Add the remaining 2 teaspoons Cajun seasoning and the Worcestershire, bring to a boil, and cook until the mixture thickens, 6 to 8 minutes. Remove from the heat and discard the bay leaf.

5. In a medium bowl, combine the shrimp, scallions, the remaining 1 teaspoon salt, and the black pepper.

6. Lightly flour your work surface and roll out the puff pastry until it's wide enough to cover the top of the skillet and overlap on the sides, about 11-inch square.

7. Add the cream and the shrimp mixture to the sauce in the skillet and stir to incorporate,

making sure the shrimp are fully submerged in the sauce.

8. In a small bowl, lightly whisk the egg with 1 tablespoon water until combined. Using a bit of this egg wash, brush the inside upper sides of the skillet, then carefully lay the puff pastry sheet over the pan, tucking the overlap under. Using a sharp paring knife, cut two ½-inch-long slits into the top of the pastry to allow steam to escape, then brush the top of the pastry with more of the egg wash.

9. Bake for 30 to 35 minutes, until the pastry is golden brown and the filling is bubbling.

10. Let rest for 10 to 15 minutes and garnish with the scallions before serving.

I'm a believer in low-key meals that still feel glorious and indulgent, and here each bite of cod feels more luxurious than the last, but the work is minimal. When you want to celebrate the smallest of achievements, like learning to change a tire or finishing a book, this is the meal, boos. I don't know anyone with a pulse who doesn't love garlic butter—a golden ticket to a surefire flavorful meal. This is a great recipe to have in your back pocket if you're hosting a small dinner party and want to save your energy for playing host. And while you wait, pour yourself a glass of wine, make a cocktail, or just kick it.

garlic butter roasted cod

SERVES 4

CELEBRATE!
A good hair day; saying yes to a new opportunity; your first successful solo tire change

5 tablespoons **unsalted butter**

7 **garlic cloves**, minced or finely grated

1 cup **cherry tomatoes**, halved

⅓ cup **white wine**

Finely grated **zest** of 1 **lime**

½ teaspoon **No-Salt Cajun Seasoning** (page 37) or store-bought

½ teaspoon **freshly ground black pepper**, plus more as needed

½ teaspoon **garlic powder**

½ teaspoon **crushed red pepper flakes**

2 tablespoons chopped **fresh cilantro**, plus more for serving

2 tablespoons chopped **fresh basil**, plus more for serving

Kosher salt

1 pound **cod**, halibut, or hake fillets

1. Position a rack in the middle of the oven and preheat to 350°F.

2. In a large ovenproof skillet, melt the butter over medium heat. When it stops foaming, add the garlic and cook, stirring, until fragrant but not burnt, about 30 seconds. Add the tomatoes and cook, stirring, until softened, 2 to 3 minutes. Stir in the wine to incorporate, then stir in the lime zest, Cajun seasoning, black pepper, garlic powder, and red pepper flakes to combine.

3. Stir in the cilantro and basil, reduce the heat to medium-low, and simmer until the sauce has

reduced by about a third, 4 to 5 minutes, then season to taste with the salt.

4. Meanwhile, pat the fish fillets dry and season both sides with salt and black pepper. Nest the fillets in the sauce and use a spoon to baste the fish with it. Cover the skillet with a lid or aluminum foil and transfer it to the oven. Bake for 10 minutes, then uncover and bake for 6 to 8 minutes more, until the fish is cooked all the way through and flakes easily with a fork. Garnish with more basil and cilantro and serve it up!

My daddy loves fried fish—and I not only inherited that love, I also passed it on to baby girl, Harmony, who asks for "fishy" twice a week. In fact, in our family, we do fish fries more than barbecue, whether it's at larger gatherings and every family reunion or as part of the weekly routine for just the immediate family. We'll take a turkey fryer and fill it with oil, then fry fish and hush puppies. It's a whole vibe, y'all.

PHOTOGRAPH ON PAGE 19

fried catfish

SERVES 4 TO 6

CELEBRATE!
Family reunion;
Friday fish fry

Nonstick cooking spray

1½ cups **fine yellow cornmeal**

½ cup **all-purpose flour**

4 teaspoons **seasoned salt**, such as Lawry's, plus more to taste

1½ teaspoons **lemon pepper**

1 teaspoon **sweet paprika**

½ teaspoon **freshly ground black pepper**

½ teaspoon **cayenne pepper**

2 large **eggs**

⅓ cup **Creole mustard** or yellow mustard

2 teaspoons **hot sauce**, plus more for serving

2 pounds **catfish**, tilapia, sea bass, whiting, or orange roughy fillets

Neutral oil, such as canola, for frying

Chopped **fresh flat-leaf parsley**, for serving

Lemon wedges, for serving

Tartar sauce, for serving

1. Coat a rimmed baking sheet with cooking spray or set a wire rack on top.

2. In a brown paper bag or large zip-top bag, combine the cornmeal, flour, seasoned salt, lemon pepper, paprika, black pepper, and cayenne. Seal the bag and shake to mix. Adjust the seasoning, if needed.

3. In a shallow medium bowl, whisk together the eggs, mustard, and hot sauce. Dip a fish fillet into the egg mixture, coating it well on both sides, then dredge it in the cornmeal mixture and shake it in the bag liberally to coat well. Place the fillet on the prepared baking sheet and repeat with the remaining fillets. Transfer the fish to the refrigerator for 10 to 15 minutes to let the coating set.

4. While the fish is chilling, fill a large Dutch oven, heavy-bottomed pot, or deep fryer with enough oil to come 4 inches up the sides and heat over medium-high heat until the oil registers about 350°F on an instant-read thermometer.

5. Working in batches, fry up that fish, turning it as needed, until golden brown, about 5 minutes. Adjust the heat as needed to keep the temperature around 350°F, and don't let it go above 375°F. Using a spider, transfer the fried fish to a paper towel–lined tray or a wire rack set over a baking sheet to drain and cool for 5 to 10 minutes. Sprinkle the parsley on top and serve with lemon wedges, hot sauce (of course), and tartar sauce on the side.

Nashville Hot–Style Catfish

½ cup **hot oil** (reserved from frying the fish;
   be careful about ladling hot oil)
2½ tablespoons **cayenne pepper**
Scant 1 tablespoon **dark brown sugar**
½ teaspoon **chili powder**
½ teaspoon **garlic powder**
½ teaspoon **smoked paprika**
¼ teaspoon **kosher salt**
Sliced white bread, for serving
Pickles, for serving

In a medium bowl, whisk together the oil, cayenne, brown sugar, chili powder, garlic powder, paprika, and salt until combined. (Be careful when whisking the hot oil, as it may splash and burn you.) Brush this mixture over the just-fried fish. Place the hot fish over slices of white bread and serve with pickles. Then get your whole life!

Rest is as essential to joy as any other ingredient, and I learned that the hard way. Until I started therapy, I didn't realize that I was aiming to be busy for busyness's sake. Sometimes the most productive thing is to stop what you're doing and recharge—you will be more productive in the long run.

This recipe can be on the table in about half an hour, letting you spend less time in the kitchen and more time just being. The best part is, it tastes so spectacular you won't even believe in took mere minutes to prep.

creamy louisiana cajun shrimp alfredo

SERVES 6

CELEBRATE! Home-alone meal (make sure you jump on the bed a few times, too!); a breakthrough in therapy

2 tablespoons **unsalted butter**
1 tablespoon **extra-virgin olive oil**
1 pound medium **shrimp**, peeled and deveined, patted dry
2½ teaspoons **No-Salt Cajun Seasoning** (page 37) or store-bought, divided, plus more for garnish

Kosher salt
8 ounces **penne**
1½ tablespoons minced or finely grated **garlic**
½ cup **heavy cream**
⅓ cup **seafood stock**, chicken stock, or vegetable stock
2 tablespoons **fresh lemon juice**, plus more to taste

⅓ cup finely chopped **fresh flat-leaf parsley**, plus more for garnish
¼ cup grated **Parmesan cheese**, plus more for garnish
1 tablespoon **fresh basil** chiffonade
½ teaspoon **onion powder**
Freshly ground black pepper

1. In a large nonstick skillet, combine the butter and olive oil over medium-high heat to melt the butter. In a bowl, toss the shrimp with 2 teaspoons of the Cajun seasoning until coated. Bring a large pot of salted water to a boil. Add the pasta and cook until al dente according to the package instructions, then drain and set aside.

2. Add the shrimp to the skillet and season with a generous pinch of salt. Cook until pink and opaque, about 2 minutes on each side. Transfer the shrimp to a bowl. Reduce the heat to medium, add the garlic, and cook until fragrant, about 30 seconds.

3. Add the cream, stock, and lemon juice and stir to combine. Stir in the parsley, Parmesan, basil, onion powder, the remaining ½ teaspoon Cajun seasoning, and black pepper to taste. Bring to a lively simmer and let the sauce thicken slightly, about 2 minutes. Return the shrimp to the skillet and stir to coat it in the sauce.

4. Reduce the heat to medium-low, then toss in the pasta, until evenly coated.

5. Divide the shrimp Alfredo among six bowls, garnish with additional Parmesan, Cajun seasoning, and parsley, and serve it up, boos.

My favorite memories of visiting my grandparents in Mississippi are the simplest ones. Many of them are about just being still, like people-watching on the front porch with a glass of sweet tea. That tea goes down smooth, keeps ya nice and alert, and cools you off. I'd add a squeeze of lemon, especially refreshing on a sweltering day. The grown-ups may have added a splash of whiskey—the caramel notes in the liquor complement the black tea flavor.

   Back then, time seemed to move slowly, and nothing was more important than just chillin' with loved ones, saying hello to passersby, and feeling the summer breeze against your neck. When you long for simpler days, this salmon, glazed with a reduction of whiskey and citrusy sweet tea, does the trick.

whiskey and sweet tea glazed salmon

SERVES 6

WHISKEY-TEA GLAZE
½ cup **whiskey**
1 **black tea bag** or 2 teaspoons loose black tea in a tea ball
¼ cup packed **dark brown sugar**
2 tablespoons **maple syrup**
½ teaspoon finely grated **lemon zest**
1½ tablespoons **fresh lemon juice** (from 1 lemon)

2 teaspoons minced **garlic**
¼ teaspoon **sweet paprika**
¼ teaspoon **freshly ground black pepper**

SALMON
1 tablespoon **canola oil**
2 pounds fresh **salmon fillets**, preferably wild-caught
1½ teaspoons **kosher salt**

1 teaspoon **freshly ground black pepper**
½ teaspoon **garlic powder**
½ teaspoon **onion powder**
¼ teaspoon **smoked paprika**
¼ teaspoon **No-Salt Cajun Seasoning** (page 37) or store-bought
⅛ teaspoon **cayenne pepper** (optional)

1. Make the whiskey-tea glaze: In a small pot, combine the whiskey with 1 cup water and bring to a boil over medium-high heat. Add the tea bag and let simmer for 2 to 3 minutes to really get that tea flavor in there. Stir in the brown sugar, maple syrup, lemon zest, lemon juice, garlic, paprika, and black pepper, then reduce the heat to medium. Simmer until the liquid starts to look like a thick syrup, about 15 minutes. Remove from the heat, discard the tea bag, and set the glaze aside.

2. Make the salmon: Position one rack in the middle of the oven and another about 6 inches away from the broiler heating element and preheat to 375°F. Line a large rimmed baking sheet with aluminum foil and grease it with the oil.

CELEBRATE!
Getting a raise;
anniversary dinner;
dog days of summer
(y'all gonna miss the
heat when it's
snowing)

3. Pat the salmon dry on both sides. In a small bowl, whisk up the salt, black pepper, garlic powder, onion powder, paprika, Cajun seasoning, and cayenne (if using) until combined.

4. Arrange the salmon skin-side down along the center of the prepared baking sheet. Sprinkle the seasoning on top of the salmon pieces, making sure to pat it in.

5. Spoon that bomb glaze over the salmon and fold up the sides of the foil to completely

enclose the fillets. (If you need more foil, just layer another piece over the top and close.) Bake for about 13 minutes, until the salmon flakes easily with a fork.

6. Remove the baking sheet from the oven and carefully open the foil pouch to expose the salmon. Switch the oven to broil and slide the baking sheet onto the top rack. Broil for about 2 minutes, until golden, then remove from the oven. Divide the salmon among six plates and serve it up right away.

If you can cook me a good meal, you've got a piece of my heart. —*jocelyn*

My husband, Frederick, has a deep love of Italian food. We joke that he's got Italian DNA somewhere. This recipe is a love letter to him—it incorporates his favorite flavors and elements. A few pantry ingredients come together in a cozy dish that's far greater than the sum of its parts. And the best thing is, it's mostly hands-off. When you want to impress your boo thang, make this! Someone might put a ring on it (just sayin'). If possible, ask your butcher to tie the roast for you; it'll help keep the meat together during cooking and will yield more tender results. *PHOTOGRAPH ON PAGE 164*

braised italian pot roast

SERVES 4 TO 10

1 (3- to 5-pound) **pot roast**
Kosher salt and **freshly ground black pepper**
3 tablespoons **extra-virgin olive oil**
1 large **yellow onion**, chopped
6 **garlic cloves**, minced or finely grated (about 2 tablespoons)

1 (28-ounce) can **crushed tomatoes**
1 (15-ounce) can **tomato sauce**
1 cup **chicken stock**
⅓ cup **dry red wine**
2 tablespoons **Italian Seasoning** (page 64) or store-bought
2 tablespoons **granulated sugar**

½ teaspoon **crushed red pepper flakes**
1 pound **rigatoni** or a similar short pasta
Grated **Parmesan cheese**, for serving
Chopped **fresh flat-leaf parsley**, for serving

1. Position a rack in the middle of the oven and preheat to 300°F.

2. Liberally season the beef all over with salt and pepper. (Don't play around here; the meat can take an assertive hand with seasoning to have lots of flavor.)

3. In a 6- to 8-quart heavy-bottomed pot or Dutch oven, warm the olive oil over medium-high heat until shimmering. Add the beef and sear until deeply browned on all sides, 15 to 20 minutes total. Transfer to a plate and set aside.

4. Scrape the bottom of the pan so all the browned bits combine with the oil. Add the onion and cook, stirring, until it starts to soften and turn golden, about 4 minutes. Add the garlic and cook, stirring, until fragrant, about 1 minute. Pour in the crushed tomatoes, tomato sauce, stock, and wine. Stir in the Italian seasoning, sugar, and red pepper flakes and season to taste with salt and black pepper. Bring the sauce to a simmer.

CELEBRATE!
The perfect
meet-the-boo-
thang's-parents meal
(sure to impress
your future in-
laws)

5. Return the meat to the pot (along with any juices accumulated on the plate) and nestle it in the sauce. Cover the pot and transfer to the oven. Cook for 3½ to 4½ hours, until the beef is tender and falling apart and the sauce has thickened.

6. Remove the pot from the oven and carefully ladle off the fat accumulated on the surface of the sauce. (If you can make this the night before and refrigerate it, the fat will solidify at the top so you can just spoon it off; otherwise, do the best you can with the liquid fat.) Set the pot over low heat and bring the sauce to a simmer. Cook, uncovered, until the sauce has thickened, 20 to 25 minutes.

7. Meanwhile, bring a large pot of salted water to a boil over high heat. Add the pasta and cook until al dente according to the package instructions, then drain. Arrange the pasta on a large serving platter.

8. Remove the meat from the sauce and, if it has been tied, discard the string. Using a sharp serrated knife, gently slice the meat across the grain (if it falls apart, that's okay). Arrange the sliced meat on top of the pasta. Generously ladle the sauce over everything, then shower with Parmesan and parsley and serve family-style.

This is a spin on one of my most popular recipes. During the summer, I can always count on my marinated skirt steak with chimichurri sauce—a guaranteed crowd-pleaser. It's tender, juicy, and bomb diggity. Bright flavors from citrus, herbs, and seasonings come together to make the steak ridiculously good. Serve it at your next grilling party—with mojitos, obviously, boos!—and watch it disappear in minutes.

mojito-marinated skirt steak with chimichurri

SERVES 4 TO 6

CELEBRATE!
Fourth of July; an engagement; "Just Got Paid" (Johnny Kemp–style); A on an exam

MOJITO-MARINATED STEAK

⅓ cup **extra-virgin olive oil**

⅓ cup **fresh lime juice** (from 2 to 3 juicy limes)

¼ cup **tamari** or soy sauce

1 cup loosely packed **fresh mint leaves**

¼ cup **fresh cilantro leaves**

½ medium **yellow onion**, coarsely chopped

4 **garlic cloves**, chopped

3 tablespoons **white vinegar**

3 tablespoons **granulated sugar**

2 tablespoons **white rum**

Juice of ½ **orange**

2 teaspoons **kosher salt**, plus more as needed

1 teaspoon **freshly ground black pepper**, plus more as needed

1 teaspoon **ground cumin**

1½ to 2 pounds **skirt steak**

CHIMICHURRI

1 cup **fresh flat-leaf parsley leaves**

1 cup **fresh cilantro leaves**

¼ cup **extra-virgin olive oil**, plus more as needed

½ medium **yellow onion**, coarsely chopped

3 **garlic cloves**, coarsely chopped

3 tablespoons **fresh lime juice**

2 tablespoons **red wine vinegar**

½ teaspoon **kosher salt**, plus more to taste

½ teaspoon **freshly ground black pepper**

¼ teaspoon **crushed red pepper flakes**

1. Marinate the steak: In a blender, combine the olive oil, lime juice, tamari, mint, cilantro, onion, garlic, vinegar, sugar, rum, orange juice, salt, black pepper, and cumin and blend until the mixture is combined but you still see small green flecks from the herbs. Transfer the marinade to a zip-top bag (or a large shallow container), add the steak, and turn it over a few times to make sure it's submerged in the marinade. If using a bag, squeeze out the excess air, seal the bag, and place it in a container large enough to hold it (to prevent possible leaks); if using a container, cover it with a lid. Transfer to the refrigerator and marinate for at least 8 hours and up to overnight.

2. When ready to grill, remove the steak from the marinade, allowing the excess to drip off, and let it come to room temperature (this will

ensure even cooking), then season liberally with more salt and black pepper.

3. Prepare a grill for direct medium heat (350° to 450°F). If using a gas grill, set it to 350°F. If using a charcoal grill, fill a chimney starter with charcoal and light it; when the coals are red hot, pour them into the grill. Add more charcoal. When all the coals have ashed over and are gray but still very hot, about 15 minutes, your grill should be medium-hot. (Use a grill thermometer or test the heat by holding your hand about 5 inches from the grill, palm down. If you can keep it there for 4 or 5 seconds, the heat should be at medium, or 350° to 450°F.)

4. Cover and grill, flipping it once midway through, until cooked to the desired doneness, 8 to 10 minutes total for medium-rare (an instant-read thermometer inserted into the thickest part of the steak should read 145°F). Transfer to a cutting board and let rest for 10 to 15 minutes before slicing.

5. Make the chimichurri: In a blender, combine the parsley, cilantro, olive oil, onion, garlic, lime juice, vinegar, salt, black pepper, and red pepper flakes and blend until combined (see Note). If the mixture is too thick, add more olive oil 1 tablespoon at a time until you reach the desired consistency. Taste and adjust the seasoning, if needed. You should have about 1 cup chimichurri.

6. Slice the steak across the grain, drizzle with the chimichurri, and serve.

note If you're making the chimichurri a few hours in advance of serving, wait to add the acidic elements (the lime juice and vinegar) until just before you're ready to serve it. Acidic ingredients turn your fresh herbs from a verdant green to a dull swampy color, and while it won't affect their taste—your steak and sauce will still be delicious—the colors won't be as bright and saturated.

CELEBRATE!
Cozy solo-
weekend project; a
birth announcement;
a sobriety
anniversary

My uncle BB is the family's "short rib king," known to spend hours on his legendary ribs, braising them until the meat falls off the bone. For years I was too intimidated to try to make ribs at any family event, but when my family and I moved to Dallas and my uncle came to visit, I decided to put my own spin on this beloved dish. After a bit of tinkering, I settled on this sweet-and-sour version, rich with pomegranate, soy sauce, brown sugar, and ginger—and Uncle BB ate two helpings. The result is so good, it's become a standard Christmas dish. Make it the night before for even better results (just reheat in the oven at 350°F for about 20 minutes).

pomegranate-ginger short ribs
SERVES 4 TO 6

3 pounds **bone-in beef short ribs** (6 or 7 ribs)
Kosher salt and **freshly ground black pepper**
3 tablespoons **extra-virgin olive oil**
1 medium **yellow onion**, chopped

3 slices **bacon**, chopped
3 **garlic cloves**, minced
2 tablespoons **all-purpose flour**
2½ cups **pomegranate juice**
1½ cups **beef stock**
⅓ cup **soy sauce**
½ cup packed **dark brown sugar**

1 tablespoon grated **fresh ginger**
1 teaspoon **ground ginger**
3 sprigs **thyme**, plus more for garnish
Pomegranate seeds, for garnish

1. Position a rack in the middle of the oven and preheat to 375°F. Set a wire rack over a large rimmed baking sheet.

2. Pat the meat dry and season it with salt and pepper. In a large pot or Dutch oven, heat the olive oil over medium-high heat until shimmering. Add the meat and sear until well browned, 2 to 3 minutes per side. Transfer to the prepared baking sheet.

3. Reduce the heat to medium and scrape the bottom of the pot to get all the delicious bits. Add the onion and bacon and cook, stirring, until the onion is tender and the bacon fat has rendered, 6 to 8 minutes. Stir in the garlic and cook for about 30 seconds. Sprinkle in the flour, stir to combine, and cook until

the mixture forms a paste, about 2 minutes. Add the pomegranate juice, stock, and soy sauce and stir to combine. Stir in the brown sugar, fresh ginger, and ground ginger until combined. Add the thyme, then bring to a boil.

4. Return the meat to the pot and cover with a large piece of parchment paper, followed by the lid. Transfer to the oven and braise for 2 to 2½ hours, until the ribs are tender and can be easily pulled apart with a fork and the liquid has thickened to a luscious sauce. Ladle out the fat on the top and discard the thyme sprigs. (If you have time, place the pot in the refrigerator overnight; the fat will solidify so you can easily scoop it out.) Serve topped with pomegranate seeds and additional thyme sprigs.

Some foods are just meant for crappy moments. Got passed over for a job opportunity? Comfort food to the rescue. And I don't eat it to wallow—I eat it to proclaim victory over the experience. Failure means I took a risk, went after a dream, and . . . welp, it didn't work out, but I did the damn thing anyway! Celebrating a win in the courage department means a rich-as-hell, creamy, cheesy, calorie-laden Philly steak mac and cheese with all the wine. It's just the ticket to get litty.

philly steak mac and cheese

SERVES 6 TO 8

CELEBRATE!
A so-called failure; getting over a breakup; the ultimate Super Bowl dish!

STEAK AND PASTA

2 teaspoons **kosher salt**, plus more as needed

2 teaspoons **freshly ground black pepper**

2 tablespoons **extra-virgin olive oil**

1 pound **rib eye steak**, sliced as thinly as possible (see Note)

½ large **yellow onion**, chopped

½ large **green bell pepper**, diced

1 **garlic clove**, minced or finely grated

2 teaspoons **Worcestershire sauce**

1 pound **cavatappi pasta**

CHEESE SAUCE AND ASSEMBLY

2 cups shredded **provolone cheese**

1½ cups shredded **mild cheddar cheese**

1 cup shredded **mozzarella cheese**

⅔ cup shredded **Parmesan cheese**

1 tablespoon **extra-virgin olive oil**

4 **garlic cloves**, minced or finely grated

3 tablespoons **unsalted butter**

¼ cup **all-purpose flour**

1½ teaspoons **onion powder**

1¼ teaspoons **garlic powder**

1 teaspoon **kosher salt**

1 teaspoon **freshly ground black pepper**

½ teaspoon **mustard powder**

½ teaspoon **sweet paprika**

¼ teaspoon **cayenne pepper**

2½ cups **heavy cream**

2½ cups **whole milk**

½ cup **panko bread crumbs**

Olive oil cooking spray or other cooking spray

2 tablespoons chopped **fresh flat-leaf parsley**, for garnish

1. Make the steak and pasta: Bring a large pot of water to a boil over high heat. In a small bowl, stir together the salt and black pepper.

2. In a large skillet, heat the olive oil over medium-high heat until shimmering. Add the steak and sear, without moving it, for 1 minute, then cook, stirring frequently, until lightly browned, about 3 minutes. Add the onion, bell pepper, and 2 teaspoons of the salt-and-pepper mixture. Cook, stirring, until all the liquid has evaporated and the steak starts to brown, 8 to 10 minutes.

3. Stir in the remaining salt-and-pepper mixture, the garlic, and the Worcestershire, remove from the heat, and set aside.

4. When the water comes to a boil, add enough salt so it tastes faintly of the sea. Add the pasta and cook until al dente according to the package instructions. Drain and set aside.

5. Position a rack in the middle of the oven and preheat to 375°F.

6. Make the cheese sauce: In a large bowl, toss together the provolone, cheddar, mozzarella, and Parmesan until combined; set aside.

7. In a large heavy-bottomed pot, heat the olive oil over medium-high heat until shimmering. Add the garlic and cook, stirring, until fragrant, about 30 seconds, then add the butter and let it melt. Quickly whisk in the flour, then cook, whisking nonstop, until a roux forms, about 1 minute. Whisk in the onion powder, garlic powder, salt, black pepper, mustard powder,

paprika, and cayenne until incorporated. Whisk in the cream and milk to combine, then whisk in half of the cheese mixture and whisk continuously until it has melted completely. Add half of the steak and all the pasta and stir to evenly coat with the cheese sauce.

8. Transfer the pasta mixture to a 9 by 13-inch baking pan with tall sides and top with the remaining steak, followed by the remaining cheese mixture. Sprinkle with the panko and spray the bread crumbs with cooking spray. Bake for 30 to 35 minutes, until the pasta is golden brown on top and some of the noodles look crispy. Remove from the oven, let cool for 10 minutes, then garnish with the parsley and serve hot.

note To slice your steak super-thin, freeze it for 2 to 3 hours, then remove it from the freezer and let it rest on the cutting board for 10 minutes. Using a very sharp knife, thinly slice across the grain.

Consider this the meal for having uncomfortable conversations. After we all watched the horrific and inhumane murder of George Floyd at the hands of police and the subsequent public outrage that followed, I had a few of these conversations with my white friends, discussing privilege, inclusion, and what it truly means to be an ally. I tried to give them a glimpse into how it felt to be the only Black woman in the room in most of my professional pursuits. When my soul grew weary from all these conversations, my mama's cooking was just the pick-me-up I needed.

I think of smothering as Southern braising, and there's no meat under the sun that Mama wouldn't smother—she taught me everything I know about it. Smothering, with its flavorful, flour-thickened sauce, moisturizes the meat, and these pork chops are the most comforting meal on a wintry night, a rainy day, or when you are just in need of a cuddle.

check yo' privilege cider-smothered pork chops

SERVES 4

6 tablespoons **vegetable oil**, divided
4 (½-inch-thick) **bone-in pork chops**
Kosher salt and **freshly ground black pepper**
½ cup plus 1 tablespoon **all-purpose flour**, divided

1 medium **yellow onion**, diced
2 **garlic cloves**, minced or finely grated
2 cups **chicken stock**
1½ cups **hard cider** or apple cider
2 tablespoons **Worcestershire sauce**

1 teaspoon **hot sauce**
½ teaspoon **No-Salt Cajun Seasoning** (page 37) or store-bought
Cooked white rice, for serving
Chopped **fresh parsley**, for garnish

1. In a large cast-iron skillet, heat 3 tablespoons of the oil over medium heat until shimmering. Set a wire rack over a baking sheet or some paper towels.

2. Pat the pork chops dry and generously season both sides with salt and pepper. Dredge the pork chops lightly in ½ cup of the flour and place in the hot skillet. Cook, without moving,

until browned on both sides, 4 to 6 minutes per side. Transfer to the rack to drain.

3. Scrape the bottom of the skillet to loosen the browned bits. Add 1 tablespoon of the oil and the onion and cook until lightly browned and softened, about 5 minutes. Add the garlic and cook until aromatic, about 1 minute.

4. Push the onion and garlic to one side of the skillet, then add the remaining 2 tablespoons oil and sprinkle in the remaining 1 tablespoon flour. Cook, stirring continuously, until the flour reaches a toffee color, 5 to 8 minutes, then pour in the stock and cider and whisk to combine.

5. Raise the heat to high and bring to a boil. Whisk in Worcestershire, hot sauce, and Cajun seasoning, then reduce the heat to medium and season to taste with salt and pepper.

6. Return the pork to the skillet, partially cover the pan, and simmer until the sauce has thickened and coats the back of a spoon, 25 to 35 minutes.

7. Divide the rice and pork chops among four plates. Spoon the sauce over both, top with chopped parsley, and serve.

CELEBRATE!
First snow of the season; Kwanzaa; a peace-offering meal after a hard convo

The cookout is the ultimate summertime gathering of Black folk. It looks a lil' something like this: spades popping off at card tables; Earth, Wind & Fire and DJ Jazzy Jeff & the Fresh Prince's "Summertime" in the background; an Electric Slide here and there; and, of course, the eats. The 'que demands the best of the best: no raisins in the potato salad, my mama's baked beans on the table, and, without any doubt, the ribs. We brine them overnight, then grill them low and slow until those babies fall off the bone. While Daddy and Uncle BB usually make traditional-style ribs, I thought Moroccan flavors would give the cookout just the bomb tribute it deserves. A barbecue glaze, doctored up with date syrup, will save you time without sacrificing taste.

moroccan ribs with bbq date glaze

SERVES 8 TO 10

CELEBRATE!
Fourth of July;
first day of summer;
the ultimate
cookout!

RIBS
8 to 10 pounds **pork baby back ribs** or beef ribs
½ cup packed **dark brown sugar**
2½ tablespoons **garlic powder**
2 tablespoons **kosher salt**
4 teaspoons **freshly ground black pepper**
4 teaspoons **smoked paprika**
1 tablespoon **ground cumin**

1 teaspoon **ground coriander**
1 teaspoon **ground cardamom**
1 teaspoon **ground allspice**
1 teaspoon **ground ginger**
1 teaspoon **ground cinnamon**
1 teaspoon **ground cloves**
1 teaspoon **freshly grated nutmeg**
½ teaspoon **ground turmeric**
½ teaspoon **cayenne pepper**
Nonstick cooking spray

BBQ GLAZE
1 (18-ounce) bottle of your favorite **barbecue sauce** (I use Sweet Baby Ray's)
½ cup **date syrup** (also known as date molasses or silan)
¼ cup **preserved lemon brine** or fresh lemon juice
2 tablespoons **apricot preserves**

1. Make the ribs: Rinse the ribs and thoroughly pat dry. Turn the rack bone-side up. Slip a sharp paring knife between the membrane and the bone, then remove the membrane. It should pull right off after you get some momentum. Set the racks on sheets of aluminum foil that will be long enough to wrap the meat.

2. In a medium bowl, whisk together the brown sugar, garlic powder, salt, black pepper, paprika, cumin, coriander, cardamom, allspice, ginger, cinnamon, cloves, nutmeg, turmeric, and cayenne until combined. Set aside 2 tablespoons of the dry rub to use in the glaze.

recipe continues

3. Spray the outside of the ribs with cooking spray and use the remaining dry rub to season the racks on both sides, massaging the mixture into the meat. Wrap the ribs tightly in the foil, set on large rimmed baking sheets (you will likely need two of them), and refrigerate for at least 6 hours and up to overnight.

4. When ready to cook the ribs, position a rack in the middle of the oven and preheat to 300°F.

5. Set the baking sheet(s) with the ribs on the counter while the oven preheats, then transfer them to the oven and slow-roast the ribs still in their foil for about 2½ hours, until the meat is tender and reaches an internal temperature of 145°F and a knife slides easily between the ribs in the thickest part and the meat.

6. Make the BBQ glaze: While the ribs are roasting, in a medium pot, combine the barbecue sauce, date syrup, preserved lemon brine, apricot preserves, and the reserved 2 tablespoons dry rub and bring to a simmer over medium heat. Reduce the heat to low and simmer, stirring occasionally, until the glaze has thickened, 10 to 15 minutes, then remove from the heat and set aside.

7. Return to the ribs: Remove the baking sheet(s) from the oven and carefully unwrap the ribs (you may want to use tongs to open the foil, and be mindful of the hot steam). Carefully drain the excess fat from the baking sheet(s), if needed, then brush the glaze all over the racks; reserve the leftover glaze for serving.

8. Position a rack about 6 inches from the broiler heating element and switch the oven to broil. Return the ribs to the oven and broil until the glaze sticks to the meat, about 2 minutes. Watch carefully, as the glaze can go from thickened to burnt in a matter of seconds. Remove from the oven and set aside for 15 minutes before carving. Serve with the remaining glaze on the side.

grilled ribs

Heat a grill to 300° to 350°F, about 10 minutes. Make sure to properly oil the grill grates so the meat won't stick, then place the marinated, uncooked ribs bone-side down on the grill over indirect heat. Cover and grill for 1½ hours, then turn the ribs over and grill, covered, still over indirect heat, for 1½ hours more, or until the meat is tender and registers 145°F on an instant-read thermometer. Try to maintain the heat as close to 300°F as you can. (If using charcoal, you will need to add more coals to maintain the temperature.) Check on the meat every now and then to make sure it doesn't stick or burn if it gets close to direct heat.

Move the ribs over direct heat and brush with the glaze on both sides. Grill, uncovered, until the glaze is sticky and thick, 5 to 10 minutes, then transfer to a serving platter, tent with aluminum foil, and let sit for about 15 minutes before serving with the remaining glaze on the side.

notes To get super-tender, smoky meat, you'll want to cook the ribs over low to medium heat. Go low and slow, baby!

Cooking meat on the grill requires constant attention. Stay close to the grill, tongs in hand like a boss, and only flip the ribs when necessary. Only baste with glaze in the last 15 minutes of cooking or the sugars will burn and the ribs might be too charred for eating.

I come from what you'd call a God-trusting-praying family. In the wake of trouble and strife, we pray. In our most glorious moments, we thank God. When my Big Daddy Sid was in his seventies, he felt God's calling to establish his church, Mt. Moriah (it's never too late to do anything in life). I've always found my grandparents' trust in Divine Providence to be awe-inspiring. Even when the road seemed tough and the answers unclear, they fully trusted God, no matter how long a prayer might take to manifest. One of my favorite acronyms, coined by Marshawn Evans Daniels, is "TRUST Is Total Reliance Upon Spiritual Timing." It's a practice I'm still working on, but there's much serenity to be gained when you let things take God's course and not allow your impatience to rush the plan. Basically, let go and let God. This oxtail dish relies on patience (we talkin' a three-hour braise, y'all), but paired with cornmeal and thyme dumplings, each bite is worth the wait.

oxtails and cornmeal dumplings

SERVES 4

CELEBRATE!
Weekly family prayer (the elders in my family have one every Sunday); winter Sunday supper

OXTAILS

4 pounds **oxtails**, trimmed of excess fat
1 tablespoon **kosher salt**, divided, plus more as needed
1 teaspoon **freshly ground black pepper**, divided, plus more as needed
¼ cup **extra-virgin olive oil**
6 slices **bacon**, chopped
2 medium **yellow onions**, chopped
2 medium **green bell peppers**, diced
2 medium **carrots**, diced
14 **garlic cloves**, minced or finely grated
2 teaspoons **chili powder**
2 teaspoons **smoked paprika**
½ teaspoon **cayenne pepper**
6 sprigs **thyme**
4 **bay leaves**
2 tablespoons **tomato paste**
¼ cup **all-purpose flour**
6 cups **beef stock**, plus more if needed
1½ cups **red wine**, plus more if needed
1½ cups **Dr Pepper**, plus more if needed
¼ cup **Worcestershire sauce**, plus more to taste
2 tablespoons **balsamic vinegar**, plus more to taste

CORNMEAL DUMPLINGS

1 cup **all-purpose flour**
½ cup **fine yellow cornmeal**
1½ teaspoons **baking powder**
1 teaspoon **kosher salt**
¼ teaspoon **freshly ground black pepper**
¼ teaspoon **dried thyme**
¾ cup well-shaken **buttermilk**
1 large **egg**, lightly beaten
2 tablespoons **unsalted butter**, melted

Fresh parsley leaves and tender stems, for serving

recipe continues

1. Make the oxtails: Position a rack in the middle of the oven and preheat to 375°F. Line a large baking sheet with paper towels or clean kitchen towels and keep it near your work area.

2. Pat the oxtails dry and liberally season with 1½ teaspoons salt and ½ teaspoon black pepper. In a large Dutch oven or heavy-bottomed pot, heat the olive oil over medium-high heat until shimmering. Add the oxtails and sear until browned on all sides, about 15 minutes total. Transfer to the prepared baking sheet and let drain.

3. Add the bacon to the pot and cook, stirring, until aromatic, about 1 minute. Add the onions, bell peppers, and carrots and cook, stirring, until tender, about 3 minutes. Stir in the garlic, the remaining 1½ teaspoons of the salt and ½ teaspoon of the black pepper, the chili powder, paprika, cayenne, thyme, and bay leaves and cook until aromatic, about 30 seconds. Stir in the tomato paste until incorporated.

4. Sprinkle in the flour and cook, stirring to incorporate, for about 2 minutes. Pour in the stock, wine, Dr Pepper, Worcestershire, and vinegar and stir until smooth.

5. Return the oxtails to the pot and bring to a lively simmer. Cover the pot with a piece of parchment paper, followed by the lid. Transfer to the oven and braise for about 2½ hours. Remove the pot from the oven, turn the oxtails over, cover with the parchment and the lid, and braise for 30 minutes more, or until the meat is completely tender and the sauce thickens and drapes those oxtails like a custom-made coat.

6. Make the cornmeal dumplings: While the oxtails are braising, in a medium bowl, whisk together the flour, cornmeal, baking powder, salt, black pepper, and thyme until combined. Stir in the buttermilk, egg, and melted butter until just combined. The batter will be thick.

7. Remove the oxtails from the oven, uncover the pot, and set on the stovetop over medium heat. Discard the bay leaves and thyme sprigs. Once the liquid begins to simmer, use a spoon to drop dollops of the cornmeal batter into the pot, spacing them out so they don't run together. If you find there's not enough liquid in the pot, add a splash more stock, wine, and Dr Pepper, tasting to ensure the proportions maintain the right balance of flavors. Season with additional Worcestershire and/or vinegar, if desired.

8. Cover the pot and reduce the heat to low. Simmer until the dumplings are cooked through and puffed, about 20 minutes. When you cut a dumpling in half, there should be no raw batter inside; if there is, return the pot to the heat, cover, and check again in 5 to 10 minutes.

9. Divide the oxtails and dumplings among four shallow bowls, sprinkle with parsley, and serve it up hot.

> In a world where we all count calories, let's count our blessings instead. —*jocelyn*

poultry

My auntie Rose is known for her over-the-top cooking. No meal, let alone Sunday supper, is basic. Dishes like this baked chicken, along with sides such as greens, candied sweet potatoes, mac and cheese, and Big Mama's rolls, are not only normal— they're *necessary*.

This family-favorite baked chicken is from her. It's mostly hands-off and comes together in minutes. We most often use wings, but you can sub in legs or thighs (no breasts!) and reduce the cooking time. If you're planning to use thighs, reduce the weight to 3 pounds, as the thighs need to be more aggressively seasoned, or keep the weight the same and slightly up the seasonings and other ingredients.

auntie's southern baked chicken

SERVES 8 TO 10

CELEBRATE!
Graduation; baby
sleeps through the
night

4 pounds **chicken wings** or
   3 pounds bone-in, skin-on
   chicken thighs or legs
2 teaspoons **seasoned salt**,
   such as Lawry's
2 teaspoons **dried rosemary**
2 teaspoons **garlic powder**

2 teaspoons **onion powder**
1 teaspoon **freshly ground
   black pepper**
⅓ cup **maple syrup**
1 large **yellow onion**, thinly
   sliced

4 tablespoons (½ stick)
   unsalted butter, cut into
   8 pieces
2 tablespoons **Worcestershire
   sauce**
Sweet paprika
Rosemary sprigs, for garnish

1. Thoroughly pat the chicken dry, transfer to a large bowl, and set aside.

2. In a small bowl, whisk together the seasoned salt, dried rosemary, garlic powder, onion powder, and pepper until combined. Sprinkle the seasoning mixture over the wings and stir to thoroughly coat the chicken with the seasoning. Cover and refrigerate for at least 2 hours and up to overnight.

3. When ready to bake, remove the chicken from the fridge and let it come to room temperature for 30 minutes. Position a rack in the middle of the oven and preheat to 325°F.

4. Place the chicken in a 9 by 13-inch baking dish. Drizzle the chicken with the maple syrup on both sides. Cover with the onion, then top it all with the pats of butter. Drizzle the Worcestershire on top, cover with aluminum foil, and bake for about 1 hour. Turn the chicken over and evenly sprinkle it with the paprika. Bake for 1 hour more, then raise the oven temperature to 350°F, remove the foil, sprinkle with more paprika, if desired, and bake for 20 to 30 minutes more, until the chicken is very tender. Garnish with the fresh rosemary and serve family-style.

When I was eight years old, my daddy took my mom and me to a fancy French restaurant. Up to that point, the only "French" things I'd eaten were fries and toast. To this day, I recall the French onion soup featuring caramelized onions in a flavorful stock and melty cheese that overwhelmed my senses in the best way possible. When I visited Paris decades later, the soup tasted as magical as I remembered. Maybe because of that memory, I associate French onion soup with epic moments, but I don't have to hop a plane to France or dress up and visit a fancy restaurant to get my fix. I decided to make a twist on the French onion soup by using chicken thighs. Those epic cheese pulls and caramelized onions are still giving what they need to give, and all those incredible flavors transport me back in time.

french onion sheet pan chicken

SERVES 6

CELEBRATE!
The night you book your flight to Paris; *Julie & Julia* movie night (I hope Julia would approve)

⅓ cup **beef stock**
2 teaspoons **Worcestershire sauce**
1 tablespoon **kosher salt**, plus more as needed
2 teaspoons **freshly ground black pepper**
2 teaspoons **smoked paprika**
3½ pounds **bone-in, skin-on chicken thighs**

3 tablespoons **extra-virgin olive oil**, divided, plus more for brushing
2 tablespoons **unsalted butter**
2 large **Vidalia onions**, thinly sliced (about 1½ pounds total)
1 teaspoon **granulated sugar**
Leaves from 3 sprigs **thyme**
⅓ cup **dry sherry**, dry vermouth, or white wine

2 tablespoons finely chopped **fresh flat-leaf parsley leaves**, plus more for garnish
4 **garlic cloves**, minced or finely grated
6 ounces shredded **Gruyère cheese**

1. Position a rack in the middle of the oven and preheat to 450°F.

2. In a small bowl, whisk together the stock and Worcestershire. In another small bowl, whisk together the salt, pepper, and paprika.

3. Thoroughly pat the chicken dry. Separate the skin from the thigh meat by inserting your index finger between the two and lifting up gently.

4. Lightly brush a large rimmed baking sheet with oil. Place the chicken on it skin-side up and brush with 2 tablespoons of the olive oil. Sprinkle generously with the seasoning mixture, both on top and beneath the skin.

5. Pour the stock mixture around the chicken (not on top), being careful not to rinse off any of the seasoning. Roast the chicken for 20 minutes.

recipe continues

6. While the chicken is cooking, in a medium skillet, heat the remaining 1 tablespoon olive oil and the butter over medium heat until the butter has melted. Add the onions and sugar, season with a couple of generous pinches of salt, cover, and cook for 15 minutes, stirring every 5 minutes and adjusting the heat as needed to prevent the onions from burning. Remove the lid and cook until the onions turn a beautiful light caramel color, another 5 minutes or so. Stir in the thyme and cook until fragrant, about 2 minutes. Remove from the heat and set aside.

7. In a small bowl, combine the sherry, parsley, and garlic. Remove the chicken from the oven and evenly pour the sherry mixture over the thighs. Evenly divide the caramelized onions over each thigh, followed by the Gruyère.

8. Return the chicken to the oven and bake for 15 minutes more, or until the cheese has fully melted. Let rest for about 5 minutes, garnish with the parsley, then serve.

With generations of family frying chicken in the South, the dish is in my blood. In Black families, the mere act of frying chicken feels celebratory. These days when I make it, I think a lot about how tedious the preparation was back then: handling and slaughtering chickens, plucking feathers and so on—clearly, an all-day affair my Big Mama excelled at. And perhaps it's the history behind generations of Black families frying chicken that makes this recipe so special. In addition to our love of fried chicken, hot sauce is a big deal in my family. My daddy is a downright hot sauce fanatic and puts it on just about everything he eats. Unsurprisingly, he loves this recipe—and if you like hot fried chicken, you will, too.

hot sauce–chipotle fried chicken

SERVES 4 TO 6

CELEBRATE!
Sunday supper; summer solstice; last day of vacay; when you find "the dress" (could be any dress)

HOT MAPLE BUTTER
4 tablespoons (½ stick) **salted butter**, at room temperature
1½ tablespoons **light brown sugar**
1½ tablespoons **maple syrup**
½ teaspoon your favorite **hot sauce**, plus more as needed
Pinch of **cayenne pepper**, plus more to taste

CHICKEN
2 cups plus 1 tablespoon well-shaken **buttermilk**, divided

2 canned **chipotle peppers in adobo sauce**
¼ cup your favorite Louisiana **hot sauce**
1 tablespoon **Worcestershire sauce**
1 teaspoon **kosher salt**
½ teaspoon **freshly ground black pepper**
6 to 8 **chicken pieces**, a mix of breasts and thighs/drumsticks (about 4 pounds)
1½ cups **all-purpose flour**

Generous ⅓ cup **cornstarch**
2½ teaspoons **kosher salt**
2½ teaspoons **smoked paprika**
1½ teaspoons **onion powder**
1½ teaspoons **garlic powder**
1½ teaspoons **Italian Seasoning** (page 64) or store-bought
¾ teaspoon **freshly ground black pepper**
¾ teaspoon **cayenne pepper**
Vegetable oil, for frying

1. Make the hot maple butter: In a medium bowl, combine the butter, brown sugar, maple syrup, hot sauce, and cayenne and, using a spatula, mix until incorporated. Taste and season with more hot sauce and/or cayenne, if you like. Cover and refrigerate until firm, about 20 minutes. Transfer the flavored butter to a piece of parchment paper and roll it into a cylinder, twisting the ends of the paper to close. Refrigerate until needed.

recipe continues

2. Make the fried chicken: In a blender or food processor, combine two cups of buttermilk, the chipotles, hot sauce, Worcestershire, salt, and black pepper and blend until smooth. Transfer the marinade to a large bowl and add the chicken, making sure to completely submerge the pieces. Cover and refrigerate for at least 5 hours and up to overnight.

3. When ready to fry, preheat the oven to 200°F. Line a large rimmed baking sheet with parchment paper; line another large rimmed baking sheet with paper towels and set a wire rack on top.

4. In a large, wide bowl, whisk together the flour, cornstarch, salt, paprika, onion powder, garlic powder, Italian seasoning, black pepper, and cayenne until combined. Drizzle the remaining 1 tablespoon buttermilk into the flour mixture and, using a fork, mix it in to create crumbs.

5. Remove the chicken from the refrigerator. Working with one piece at a time, use tongs to lift a piece of chicken from the brine, letting the excess drip back into the bowl, and transfer to the bowl with the flour mixture. Dredge in the flour mixture, using a spoon to help you, if necessary, until the chicken is thoroughly coated. Transfer to the baking sheet lined with parchment and repeat with the remaining pieces. Let sit at room temperature for about 20 minutes to allow the coating to adhere. (This rest brings the chicken closer to room temperature, which means more even cooking, and helps the coating stay on the meat instead of puffing and pulling away from the chicken during frying.)

6. Fill a large cast-iron skillet with tall sides or a Dutch oven with oil to a depth of about ¾ inch. Heat over medium heat until the oil registers 350°F on an instant-read thermometer. (If using a cast-iron skillet, have a splatter guard nearby.)

7. Working in batches to avoid overcrowding the pan, gently slide a few chicken pieces into the hot oil. Fry the chicken until golden brown, about 8 minutes per side; the internal temperature of the chicken should be 165°F. Transfer the cooked chicken to the baking sheet with the wire rack to drain, then transfer the pan to the oven to keep warm while you fry the remaining chicken.

8. To serve, divide the chicken among the plates and top with the hot maple butter.

notes Ever wonder what to do with the remaining chipotles in adobo after you've opened a whole can? If you don't anticipate using them soon, divide them into smaller containers, label them with the date, and freeze until needed.

We most certainly reuse frying oil in my family. My mama taught me not to waste a dang-on thing, so we wait until it has cooled completely after frying, then pour it into a canister, using a funnel to avoid spills, and save it for the next time we fry. If you store it for longer than a week, refrigerate it; otherwise, room temperature is fine. I usually won't use the same oil more than twice (or up to three times if I lightly fry).

This recipe is dedicated to my best friend, Leonore. She was one of the most fun people I've ever met, and she tragically died in a senseless drive-by shooting in Chicago less than an hour after we saw one another at an event. Even typing this many years later still feels surreal, because it seemed like she'd be around forever. Each time we got together, ridiculous laughter ensued. And it usually happened over anything covered in copious amounts of melted cheese. It felt only right to honor Leonore with a meal she would have loved, even though she would ask for even more cheese. I miss her and our cheese-laden dates every day.

ancho turkey and mustard greens enchiladas

SERVES 4

ANCHO CHILE SAUCE
3 **ancho chiles**, seeded
2¼ cups hot **chicken stock**, divided
2 tablespoons **extra-virgin olive oil**
1 medium **white onion**, diced
½ medium **red onion**, diced
5 **garlic cloves**, minced or finely grated
1 small handful **fresh cilantro**
1 tablespoon **tomato paste**
1 tablespoon **red wine vinegar**
1 tablespoon **fresh lime juice**

2 teaspoons **dried oregano**, preferably Mexican
1½ teaspoons **kosher salt**
1 teaspoon **ground cumin**
1 teaspoon **smoked paprika**
1 teaspoon **freshly ground black pepper**

ENCHILADAS
1 bunch **mustard greens**, leaves stemmed and sliced into thin ribbons
2 tablespoons **extra-virgin olive oil**, plus more for greasing
1 pound **ground turkey**
¼ cup **chicken stock**

1 teaspoon **kosher salt**
12 **corn tortillas**, warmed in a lightly greased skillet
1½ cups shredded **queso quesadilla** (quesadilla cheese) or a mix of cheddar and Jack cheeses

TO SERVE
Diced **red onion**
2 medium **tomatoes**, chopped
Fresh cilantro
Crema or sour cream (optional)
Sliced **avocado** (optional)
Lime wedges (optional)

1. Make the sauce: Heat a large skillet over medium-high heat until hot. Add the chiles and toast for 30 to 45 seconds, then turn over and repeat. Watch carefully, because we just want to add a nice toasty char to the chiles without burning them. They will puff up a bit, and that's what we wanna see. Transfer the chiles to a medium pot and cover with 1¼ cups of the hot stock; set aside.

recipe continues

2. Reduce the heat under the skillet to medium and add the olive oil, followed by the white and red onions. Cook, stirring frequently, until tender, 5 to 6 minutes, then stir in the garlic and cook until barely aromatic, just 10 seconds. Remove from the heat and transfer to a blender.

3. Add the toasted chiles along with the infused stock, the cilantro, tomato paste, vinegar, lime juice, oregano, salt, cumin, paprika, and pepper to the blender. Add the remaining 1 cup stock and blend until the mixture is smooth and incorporated.

4. **Make the enchiladas:** Bring a medium pot of water to a boil over high heat. Fill a large bowl with ice and water. Add the mustard greens to the boiling water and blanch until softened, about 5 minutes. Using a slotted spoon, move the greens to the ice bath and let cool for 5 minutes. Drain and squeeze out excess water from the greens.

5. In a large skillet (you can use the same one you used for the sauce), heat the olive oil over medium heat until shimmering. Add the turkey and cook, stirring and breaking it up with a wooden spoon, until no longer pink, 5 to 7 minutes. Add the mustard greens, stock, and salt and stir to combine. Reduce the heat to medium-low, cover, and simmer until the greens are tender and deep green, about 6 minutes. Remove from the heat, stir in ½ cup of the ancho chile sauce, and let cool completely.

6. When you are ready to assemble the enchiladas, position a rack in the middle of the oven and preheat to 350°F. Grease a 9 by 13-inch baking dish with a little olive oil.

7. Evenly spread ½ cup of the ancho sauce on the bottom of the prepared dish. Add 1 to 2 tablespoons of the prepared turkey-greens filling to the center of a tortilla, roll it up, and place it seam-side down in the baking dish. Repeat with the remaining tortillas, stacking the filled tortillas next to one another in the baking dish as you go. (You may have about 1 cup of the turkey-greens mixture left over; save it for another use.) Evenly pour the remaining sauce over the tortillas, top with the cheese, and cover with aluminum foil. Bake for about 15 minutes, then remove the foil and bake for 5 to 10 minutes more, until the cheese is melty deliciousness.

8. **To serve:** Garnish with red onion, tomatoes, and cilantro. Serve it up family-style, with crema, avocado, and lime wedges on the side, if desired.

notes If you can't find mustard greens, which have a unique, hard-to-imitate flavor, you can sub in kale, but the flavor profile will change.

To reheat leftover enchiladas, preheat the oven to 350°F and grease a baking dish with a little oil. Place the enchiladas in the dish, cover with a piece of aluminum foil, and bake for about 20 minutes, uncovering the dish for the last 5 to 10 minutes of baking.

CELEBRATE!
Work promotion; completing a major goal; doing something nice for your bestie just because

Everyone needs a bomb whole chicken recipe, and this checks all the boxes: herby, citrusy, multilayered goodness, with juicy meat and crispy skin from the "brick" technique—basically what dreams are made of. Don't speed through marinating, as it will make your chicken more flavorful.

citrus cuban mojo brick chicken

SERVES 4

CELEBRATE! Treating the boss to dinner; your kid in the school play; keeping a plant alive for a year

MARINADE

⅔ cup chopped **fresh cilantro**

Finely grated **zest and juice of** 2 **lemons**

Finely grated **zest and juice of** 2 **limes**

Finely grated **zest and juice of** 1 **orange**

1 medium **yellow onion,** quartered

6 **garlic cloves**

Scant ½ cup **apple cider vinegar**

3 tablespoons **dark brown sugar**

2 tablespoons **extra-virgin olive oil**

2 tablespoons **tamari**

1 tablespoon chopped **fresh oregano leaves**

1½ teaspoons **ground cumin**

1½ teaspoons **kosher salt**

1 teaspoon **smoked paprika**

1 teaspoon **Worcestershire sauce**

½ teaspoon **freshly ground black pepper**, plus more to taste

½ teaspoon **No-Salt Cajun Seasoning** (page 37) or store-bought

⅛ teaspoon **cayenne pepper**

CHICKEN

1 (4-pound) **whole chicken,** neck and giblets removed

Kosher salt and **freshly ground black pepper**

Extra-virgin olive oil, for brushing the chicken

2 **heavy bricks,** wrapped in aluminum foil, or another heavy pan, such as a cast-iron skillet

¼ cup **honey**

1 tablespoon **fresh lime juice**

1 tablespoon **apple cider vinegar**

Fresh cilantro leaves, for garnish

1. Make the marinade: In a blender, combine the cilantro, citrus zests and juices, onion, garlic, vinegar, brown sugar, olive oil, tamari, oregano, cumin, salt, paprika, Worcestershire, black pepper, Cajun seasoning, and cayenne and pulse until completely smooth. You should get about 2 cups of marinade; measure out ⅓ cup of the marinade and refrigerate until needed. Set the remaining marinade aside.

2. Prepare the chicken: Using kitchen shears, cut out the backbone of the chicken. Pierce the chicken skin and flesh all over, outside and inside, with a sharp paring knife. Place the chicken in a large zip-top plastic bag and pour the marinade over it, making sure the chicken

recipe continues

is completely submerged. Squeeze the excess air out of the bag, seal, and refrigerate for at least 8 hours and up to 12 hours. Don't skimp here!

3. When ready to cook, position a rack in the middle of the oven and preheat to 425°F.

4. Remove the chicken from the marinade and liberally season the bird all over with salt and black pepper (discard the marinade in the bag). Brush the chicken skin all over with the olive oil.

5. Heat a large ovenproof skillet (preferably cast iron) over high heat until hot and just starting to smoke. Place the chicken breast-side down in the pan, then set the foil-wrapped bricks or heavy skillet on top to weight it down. Sear until nicely browned, about 3 minutes.

6. Transfer the chicken, still weighted down, to the oven and roast for 23 to 25 minutes. Remove the bricks or pan, flip the chicken over, and roast, uncovered, for 5 to 10 minutes more, until an instant-read thermometer inserted into the thickest part of the thigh registers 165°F.

7. Meanwhile, combine the reserved ⅓ cup marinade with the honey, lime juice, and vinegar and whisk until fully incorporated.

8. Remove the chicken from the oven and brush it with the marinade mixture. Set a rack 6 inches away from the broiler heating element and switch the oven to broil. Return the chicken to the oven and let it crisp up under the broiler for 1 to 2 minutes—watch the chicken carefully, as it can go from charred perfection to burnt to a crisp in seconds. Remove the chicken from the oven, transfer to a cutting board, and let rest for about 15 minutes before carving, garnishing with the cilantro, and serving.

note If you have any leftover marinade, you can add it to the skillet you used for roasting the chicken (but don't touch that skillet without oven mitts, boos—it's red hot) and bring it to a lively simmer on the stovetop over medium heat. Cook until the glaze thickens, 2 to 3 minutes. Remove from the heat and throw in a tablespoon or two of unsalted butter and stir to melt. Instant sauce, boos!

CELEBRATE!
First day of winter;
a cold Sunday
supper; first-date
anniversary!

When the temps dip below freezing, I reward myself with a bowl of this stew. The bold flavors of the North African harissa, made from red chiles and warm spices, intensify as the ingredients simmer together, resulting in a fragrant and comforting meal. Get cozy by the fireplace while you enjoy each bite.

harissa chicken chickpea stew

SERVES 6

3½ teaspoons **kosher salt**, divided

2½ teaspoons **freshly ground black pepper**, divided

1 teaspoon **smoked paprika**

1 tablespoon plus 1 teaspoon **garlic powder**, divided

3½ teaspoons **ground cinnamon**, divided

6 **bone-in, skin-on chicken thighs**

4 tablespoons **extra-virgin olive oil**, divided

½ cup **harissa** (hot or mild)

½ cup **maple syrup**

½ cup **preserved lemon brine**

½ cup **low-sodium chicken stock**

2 tablespoons **tomato paste**

2 tablespoons **coconut milk**

1 tablespoon **tamari** or soy sauce

1 teaspoon **crushed red pepper flakes**

1 medium **yellow onion**, diced

4 **garlic cloves**, minced or finely grated

3 sprigs **thyme**

2 **bay leaves**

2 tablespoons **all-purpose flour**

1 (14.5-ounce) can **diced tomatoes with their juices**

1 (15.5-ounce) can **chickpeas**, drained and rinsed

12 ounces **cauliflower florets** (about 2½ cups)

Chopped **fresh flat-leaf parsley**, for serving

1. In a small bowl, whisk together 2 teaspoons of the salt, 1½ teaspoons of the black pepper, the paprika, 1 teaspoon of the garlic powder, and 1 teaspoon of the cinnamon. Pat the chicken dry and season with the spice mixture.

2. In a large Dutch oven, heat 1 tablespoon of the olive oil over medium-high heat until shimmering. Working in batches, if necessary, add the chicken, skin-side down, and cook until golden brown, about 3 minutes per side, then transfer to a plate.

3. In a medium bowl, whisk together the remaining 3 tablespoons olive oil, harissa, maple syrup, preserved lemon brine, stock, tomato paste, coconut milk, remaining salt, 1 teaspoon black pepper, 1 tablespoon garlic powder,

2½ teaspoons cinnamon, the tamari, and red pepper flakes until combined.

4. In the Dutch oven, add the onion and cook, stirring, until softened, about 3 minutes. Stir in the garlic, thyme, and bay leaves and cook for about 30 seconds. Stir in the flour to incorporate. Add the harissa mixture, tomatoes, chickpeas, and cauliflower and stir to combine.

5. Return the chicken and any accumulated juices to the pot and bring the mixture to a lively simmer. Reduce the heat to low, cover, and cook until the chicken is cooked through and the cauliflower is tender, about 30 minutes. Discard the bay leaves. Divide the stew among six shallow bowls, shower with a lil' parsley, and serve it up.

How often do we celebrate the gift of wisdom and maturity? In the past, I was all too ready to throw verbal 'bows just to prove I was right (I played no games). But these days, I'm more interested in protecting my peace and my chi while keeping my sassy, spicy personality in check, and to celebrate it, this zingy ginger beer chicken in peri-peri spices is just the ticket. It starts with a painstakingly developed spice rub, then the chicken is set atop a can of ginger beer, which keeps the meat moist and infuses it with flavor. Choose your own adventure in how you want to cook it: roast or grill. Already dope on its own, the chicken gets its final glow-up with a homemade peri-peri sauce, and boos, the result? Explosive! Flavor magnetic! On point! A reminder that my fiery attitude still reigns supreme, but I just have to check her every once in a while.

peri-peri ginger beer chicken

SERVES 4

CHICKEN
2 tablespoons **garlic powder**
1 tablespoon **smoked paprika**
1 tablespoon **dried oregano**
1 tablespoon **onion powder**
1 tablespoon **kosher salt**
2 teaspoons **granulated sugar**
1 teaspoon **cayenne pepper**
1 teaspoon **ground coriander**
1 teaspoon **ground cardamom**
1 teaspoon **freshly grated nutmeg**
1 teaspoon **ground ginger**
1 teaspoon **freshly ground black pepper**

1 (4-pound) **whole chicken**, neck and giblets removed, patted dry

PERI-PERI SAUCE
2 teaspoons **smoked paprika**
2 teaspoons **kosher salt**
1 teaspoon **cayenne pepper**
1 teaspoon **granulated sugar**
1 teaspoon **dried oregano**
5 tablespoons **extra-virgin olive oil**, divided
2 large **red bell peppers**, seeded and sliced
1 large **red onion**, chopped
1 **red serrano chile**, seeded

6 **garlic cloves**
1 teaspoon **peri-peri chile seasoning**, such as Robertsons
Finely grated **zest of 1 lemon**
¼ cup **fresh lemon juice** (from 2 lemons)
¼ cup **red wine vinegar**
3 **bay leaves**
Leaves from 2 sprigs **rosemary**, plus sprigs for garnish
½ teaspoon **freshly ground black pepper**
1 (12-ounce) can **ginger beer** or ginger ale

1. Brine the chicken: In a small bowl, combine the garlic powder, paprika, oregano, onion powder, salt, sugar, cayenne, coriander, cardamom, nutmeg, ginger, and black pepper.

Season the chicken all over with this seasoning mix, including inside the cavity (get in there!). Tie the legs together with butcher's twine (this is optional, boos, but makes for a prettier

recipe continues

CELEBRATE!
Growth! Being
the bigger person;
in vitro success (as an
IVF mommy, I know
what a huge deal
this is!)

presentation) and set the chicken on a small baking sheet. Transfer to the fridge to brine, uncovered, for at least 4 hours and up to overnight.

2. Make the peri-peri sauce: In a small bowl, stir together the paprika, salt, cayenne, sugar, and oregano and slide to the side.

3. In a large skillet, heat 2 tablespoons of the olive oil over medium-high heat until shimmering. Add the bell peppers, onion, and serrano and cook, stirring occasionally, until the vegetables have a slight char, 8 to 10 minutes. Add the garlic and cook until aromatic, about 1 minute.

4. Transfer the mixture, including any liquid in the pan, to a blender or food processor, add the spice mix, peri-peri, lemon zest, lemon juice, vinegar, bay leaves, rosemary, black pepper, and the remaining 3 tablespoons olive oil and blend until smooth. Transfer the mixture to a medium pot and bring to a simmer over medium-low heat. Cook, stirring occasionally, until the sauce darkens and thickens slightly and the flavors meld, 8 to 10 minutes. Remove from the heat, discard the bay leaves, and set aside.

5. Roast the chicken: Remove the chicken from the fridge and let it chillax on the counter for about 30 minutes—this will ensure more even cooking. Position a rack in the bottom third of the oven and preheat to 400°F.

6. Open the ginger beer and pour about half of it into a glass. Have a drink or make a cocktail with it. You deserve it! Place the half-filled can in the middle of a baking pan and carefully slide the seasoned chicken over the can so it stands upright. Carefully slide the pan into the oven and roast for 1 hour, then rotate the pan front to back and roast for 10 minutes more. Remove from the oven and brush a thick layer of the peri-peri sauce over the chicken. Roast for 10 minutes more, or until the thickest part of the thigh registers 160°F on an instant-read thermometer. Transfer the baking pan to a wire rack and let rest for 10 minutes.

7. While the chicken is resting, pour the remaining peri-peri sauce into a medium pot. Bring to a simmer over medium heat and cook, stirring occasionally, until thickened, 5 to 7 minutes. Remove from the heat.

8. Carefully remove the can from the chicken; both will be extremely hot, so hold the chicken with a pair of tongs and slide the can out using another pair of tongs. Let sit for 5 minutes, then carve the chicken and transfer to a serving platter. Garnish with the rosemary and serve the chicken pieces with that delectable peri-peri sauce. You might wanna put it on EVERYTHING!

When it comes to Thanksgiving turkey, my daddy usually handles things, and he loves to fry it up! He starts by injecting a homemade Cajun-spiced seasoning directly into the meat, letting it flavor the bird for two days before the skin is seasoned to the gods with a spicy, savory rub. Finally, the whole thing is dipped into a bath of hot oil and brought to the table golden—almost the color of caramel—moist, and glorious. I believe a roasted bird can be just as sublime if done correctly. This one ticks the boxes, with deep, bright flavors, thanks to a dry brine of salt, sugar, and citrus zest. Roasted with an herby butter rubdown and a good-ass brush-down of tamarind glaze, this roasted turkey gives my fave fried bird a run for its money.

tamarind and hot honey glazed turkey

SERVES 8 TO 10

TURKEY
1 (11- to 12-pound) **whole turkey**, preferably pasture-raised, thawed if frozen
¼ cup packed **light brown sugar**
3 tablespoons **kosher salt**
1 small **orange**, finely zested and cut into wedges
1 **lemon**, finely zested and cut into wedges

2 cups **low-sodium chicken stock**, plus more as needed
1 large **onion**, cut into wedges
6 **garlic cloves**, divided
7 sprigs **rosemary**, divided
1 tablespoon finely chopped **fresh thyme leaves**
1 tablespoon finely chopped **fresh sage**
4 tablespoons (½ stick) **unsalted butter**, at room temperature

GLAZE
1 cup **fresh orange juice** (from about 2 oranges)
⅓ cup **honey**
2 tablespoons **tamarind paste**
2 tablespoons **unsulfured molasses**
2 tablespoons **sriracha**
2 tablespoons **soy sauce**
1 tablespoon **Worcestershire sauce**
1 tablespoon grated **fresh ginger**
2 **garlic cloves**, minced or finely grated

CELEBRATE!
Any holiday;
when family comes
to town or when your
kids are home from
college

recipe continues

1. Brine the turkey: Two days before you plan to serve the turkey, remove the bird from its packaging and set aside the giblets and neck. If it comes with a pop-up thermometer, discard that. Thoroughly pat the turkey dry with paper towels. Set a wire rack on a large rimmed baking sheet and put the turkey on the rack.

2. In a small bowl, whisk together the sugar, salt, and the orange and lemon zests. Generously season the turkey all over with the sugar mixture, including seasoning under the skin in the breast area and inside the cavity (get all up in there, boos). Treat the turkey like it's at a spa and you're giving it a massage.

3. Clear an entire shelf in your fridge so the turkey can chill-mode in there for a few days. You won't want anything touching that raw meat, so do take care. If you absolutely cannot afford the fridge space (I get it!), you can loosely tent the bird with some aluminum foil to prevent contact. Cover the turkey with foil and refrigerate for 24 hours, turning it over halfway through. Remove the foil and set it aside (you'll need it for roasting the next day); refrigerate the bird for another 24 hours to let the skin dry out. That uncovered rest will get you the most shatteringly crispy, delectable skin, and we know that's the best part of the turkey!

4. When you are ready to roast your bird, remove it from the refrigerator and let it come to room temperature for about 1 hour—that will ensure the turkey cooks more evenly, which is key! Position a rack in the lower third of the oven and preheat to 450°F. Set a wire rack in a large roasting pan.

5. Pour the stock into the pan. Scatter half of the onion, 3 of the garlic cloves, and 3 of the rosemary sprigs in the stock. Tuck the remaining onion, 2 of the garlic cloves, and 2 of the rosemary sprigs in the turkey cavity. Tuck a few citrus wedges in the cavity as well.

6. Mince the remaining 2 rosemary sprigs, the thyme, sage, and remaining garlic clove. Transfer to a medium bowl, add the butter, and mash them together until incorporated. Rub the compound butter all over the turkey and under its skin. (The bonus of having extra-dry skin now is that the butter ain't gonna slide off!)

7. Set the turkey on the rack and roast with the legs facing the back of the oven for about 20 minutes; at this point, the skin should be generously blistered. Remove the turkey from the oven and reduce the oven temperature to 350°F. Tent the entire turkey with the large piece of foil you used earlier. Stick a probe thermometer into the thickest part of the thigh—without touching the bone—and return the turkey to the oven. Set the probe thermometer to go off when it reaches 130°F—this should take 45 to 55 minutes.

8. Make the glaze: In a medium saucepan, combine the orange juice, honey, tamarind, molasses, sriracha, soy sauce, Worcestershire, ginger, and garlic. Cook over medium heat, stirring occasionally, until the glaze reduces by about half and thickens to a sticky syrup, about 15 minutes. Remove from the heat and set aside. You should have a scant 1 cup glaze.

9. When the turkey's internal temperature reaches 130°F, start brushing the turkey with that glorious glaze every 15 minutes and roast until the turkey's internal temperature reaches 161°F, 30 to 45 minutes more total. Remove the turkey from the oven, loosely tent it with foil, and let rest for 20 to 30 minutes before carving. During the rest time, the temperature of the turkey will continue to climb and will reach a safe 165°F.

note The general rule of thumb is 1 tablespoon of kosher salt per 4 pounds of turkey (this also applies to chicken, duck, goose, etc.). If using table salt or fine sea salt, go with half that amount, so 1½ teaspoons of salt per 4 pounds of turkey.

> Don't settle for the crumbs in life—eat the whole cake! —*jocelyn*

desserts

As a lil' girl, I always looked forward to my mama making her pineapple upside-down cake, one of her specialties. My eyes would stare in wonder as she flipped her cast-iron skillet over, revealing that syrupy pineapple wonder with its ruby-colored cherries peeking through. I loved a slice served warm, when those juices were very much still seeping into the luscious, moist vanilla cake, served with whipped cream, of course. Every time she made this, it felt like a reason to celebrate. Here I took all the elements I love in a pineapple upside-down cake and deconstructed it, revamping it into an old-school punch bowl cake (or trifle, as you might know it). The best part is, you can grab leftover vanilla cake, yellow cake layers, or even a couple of store-bought pound cakes to make this beauty. Do you, boos! It will save you some time so you can work on the juicy candied pineapples, heavenly coconut–cream cheese buttercream, tart cherry compote, and citrusy spiced cinnamon-lime whipped cream.

pineapple upside-down punch bowl cake

MAKES 1 CAKE (SERVES 16)

PINEAPPLE
⅓ cup (75 grams) **unsalted butter**
⅓ cup packed (73 grams) **dark brown sugar**
1 **pineapple** (get a Maui Gold, if you can), trimmed and cut into bite-size pieces
¼ cup **dark rum**
2 teaspoons **vanilla extract**
1 teaspoon **fresh lime juice**

COCONUT-CREAM CHEESE BUTTERCREAM
½ cup (1 stick/113 grams) **unsalted butter**, at room temperature

2 (8-ounce/227-gram) packages **cream cheese**, somewhat softened but still a little stiff
3½ cups (438 grams) **confectioners' sugar**, sifted
¼ teaspoon **kosher salt**
1½ teaspoons **coconut extract**
1 teaspoon **vanilla extract**

CHERRIES
⅔ cup (133 grams) **granulated sugar**
½ cup (45 grams) **cornstarch**
½ cup **cherry liqueur** or fresh orange juice (from 2 oranges)

7 cups quartered **pitted cherries** or 2 pounds (908 grams) frozen cherries (no need to defrost)

TO ASSEMBLE
2 (8 by 4-inch) loaves **vanilla pound cake**, cut into 1-inch cubes
2 cups cold **heavy cream**
6 tablespoons sifted **confectioners' sugar**
1 teaspoon finely grated **lime zest**, plus more for garnish, and 2 tablespoons fresh **lime juice** (from 1 lime)
1 teaspoon **ground cinnamon**
¼ teaspoon **kosher salt**

recipe continues

CELEBRATE!
Closing on a new
house (make this your
first dessert in that
new kitchen)

1. **Prepare the pineapple:** In a large skillet, melt the butter over medium heat, then stir in the brown sugar and melt both together. Add the pineapple, arranging it in as much of an even layer as possible in the skillet. Cook, without stirring, until browned on the bottom, 3 to 4 minutes, then flip and cook until browned on the other side, another 1 to 2 minutes.

2. Pour the rum, vanilla, and lime juice over the pineapple and cook, stirring occasionally, until the liquid thickens, 10 to 12 minutes. Turn off the heat and let cool completely.

3. **Make the coconut–cream cheese buttercream:** In the bowl of a stand mixer fitted with the whisk attachment, beat the butter and cream cheese on high speed until thick and fluffy, about 3 minutes. Reduce the mixer speed to its lowest setting, carefully add the confectioners' sugar, and mix until incorporated. Scrape down the sides and bottom of the bowl, making sure to incorporate all the confectioners' sugar, then whip on high until the frosting is fluffy, about 4 minutes. Stop the mixer, add the salt, coconut extract, and vanilla, and beat on high until smooth. Transfer to another bowl, cover, and chillax in the fridge until ready to assemble the cake. (You can wash out the mixer bowl and use it to make the whipped cream.)

4. **Prepare the cherries:** In a medium pan, combine the granulated sugar, cornstarch, and liqueur and cook over medium heat, stirring, until the sugar begins to melt. Add the cherries and stir until coated in the sugar mixture, then bring to a simmer. Cook until the cherries begin to release their juices and soften, about 15 minutes for frozen cherries (adjust the time accordingly if using fresh or defrosted cherries). Remove from the heat and let cool completely—the liquid will continue to thicken as it cools.

5. **Assemble the cake:** Arrange half of the cake cubes over the bottom of a 4-quart trifle dish or glass serving bowl. Layer with half of the pineapple, making sure to soak the cake with the liquid. Evenly distribute half of the cherry compote over the pineapples and top by evenly spreading half of the buttercream. Repeat the layering once more, reversing the order of the buttercream and cherry compote, then cover with plastic wrap and pop it in the fridge for at least 3 hours or up to overnight.

6. Just before serving, in a cold bowl and using a cold whisk (or in the bowl of the stand mixer fitted with the whisk attachment), whip the heavy cream on medium-high speed until medium peaks form. Add the confectioners' sugar, lime zest, lime juice, cinnamon, and salt and whip until stiff peaks form, 2 to 3 minutes. Spread the whipped cream directly over the top of the trifle, garnish with lime zest, and dig in!

My carrot cake became a viral sensation after it won *The Kitchn*'s carrot cake recipe showdown against some heavy hitters: King Arthur Baking, *Cook's Illustrated*, and the queen herself, Ina Garten. Seemingly overnight, the cake became the ultimate celebration dessert, with everyone on social media making it for everything from birthdays to holidays. What sets my carrot cake apart from others is the brown butter in the cream cheese frosting, which lends the cake a deeper, nutty flavor and makes it truly special. While this cake is a natural choice for Easter, it's also an excellent option for a grown-up birthday cake.

THE *carrot cake*

MAKES ONE 9-INCH THREE-LAYER CAKE
(SERVES 16)

CELEBRATE!
Easter; retirement;
seeing the first
flowers of spring

CARROT CAKE
Shortening, for greasing the pans
2½ cups (313 grams) **self-rising flour** (see Note), plus more for dusting
1½ teaspoons **ground cinnamon**
1 teaspoon **baking soda**
½ teaspoon **freshly grated nutmeg**
½ teaspoon **ground cloves**
½ teaspoon **kosher salt**
¼ teaspoon **ground allspice**
2 cups (400 grams) **granulated sugar**

1 cup (210 grams) **vegetable oil**
1 tablespoon **vanilla extract** or vanilla paste
4 large **eggs**, at room temperature
3 cups (330 grams) grated **carrots** (about 6 medium)
½ cup (90 grams) crushed **pineapple**, partially drained (optional)
1 cup (120 grams) chopped **toasted walnuts** (optional)

BROWN BUTTER–CREAM CHEESE FROSTING
½ cup (1 stick/113 grams) **unsalted butter**, at room temperature
2 (8-ounce/227-gram) packages **cream cheese**, somewhat softened but still a little stiff
3½ cups (440 grams) unsifted **confectioners' sugar**, plus more as needed (see Note)
1 teaspoon **vanilla extract**
Pinch of **kosher salt**

1. Make the carrot cake: Position a rack in the middle of the oven and preheat to 350°F. Line the bottoms of three 9-inch round cake pans with parchment paper cut to fit, then lightly grease the pans and parchment with shortening and dust with a little flour, tapping out any excess.

2. In a large bowl, whisk together the flour, cinnamon, baking soda, nutmeg, cloves, salt, and allspice and set aside.

3. In the bowl of a stand mixer fitted with the paddle attachment, beat the granulated sugar,

recipe continues

oil, and vanilla on medium speed until light and fluffy, about 3 minutes. Add the eggs one at a time, stopping and scraping down the bottom and sides of the bowl to completely incorporate each egg before adding the next.

4. Reduce the mixer speed to low and add the flour mixture in three increments. Mix until just combined. Remove the bowl from the mixer and fold in carrots, pineapple (if desired), and walnuts (if using).

5. Divide the batter evenly among the prepared cake pans; each pan should get between 500 and 550 grams of batter. Either jiggle the pans or use an offset spatula to smooth out the tops. Bake for 35 to 40 minutes, until a toothpick inserted into the center comes out clean. (I usually bake two pans at once, then bake the third pan once the first two are done. If you have an oven that fits all three cake pans at once, by all means bake them at the same time.) Transfer the pans to wire racks and let cool for 10 minutes, the gently flip the cakes out onto the racks and let cool completely.

6. **Make the brown butter–cream cheese frosting:** In a small saucepan, melt the butter over medium heat until white foam appears on the surface, then watch carefully as the butter solids change from yellow to brown and it starts to smell nutty. Remove from the heat and transfer the saucepan to the refrigerator. Let cool until the butter returns to a solid form, 45 minutes to 1 hour.

7. In the bowl of a stand mixer fitted with the paddle attachment, beat the cooled brown butter and the cream cheese on high speed until the mixture begins to thicken, about 5 minutes. Reduce the speed to low and add the confectioners' sugar. Beat until completely incorporated, then raise the mixer speed to high and beat until smooth. Add the vanilla and salt and beat again until the frosting is smooth.

8. To assemble the cake, use a large serrated knife or cake leveler to trim the top of each layer to make sure they are level. Reserve the nicest-looking layer to top the cake.

9. Place one of the other cake layers cut-side up on a cake plate or flat round platter. Place about 1 cup of the frosting in the center of the cake and use an offset spatula to spread it evenly to the edges. Place a second cake layer cut-side up directly on top of the first, making sure the edges line up. Place about 1 cup of the frosting in the center of the cake and spread it evenly to the edges. Top with the third cake layer, cut-side down, and press down gently to secure it. Place about 1 cup of the frosting in the center of the cake and spread it in a thin layer all over the top and as much of the sides as you can get. Use additional frosting to cover the sides of the cake in a thin layer of frosting—this is your crumb coat, which helps trap any cake crumbs in place, resulting a stunning, smoothly iced cake later. Transfer the cake (and the remaining frosting) to the refrigerator and let the crumb coat set for about 30 minutes.

10. When the crumb coat is no longer sticky to the touch, use an offset spatula to generously frost the top and sides of the cake with the remaining frosting, moving the spatula in a figure-eight motion to create swirls. Refrigerate the cake for at least 30 minutes before serving to let the frosting set up. You can also refrigerate the cake overnight, then leave it out on the counter for about 30 minutes before serving.

notes If you need to make your own self-rising flour, for every 1 cup (125 grams) of all-purpose flour, add 1½ teaspoons baking powder and ¼ teaspoon kosher salt; whisk to combine.

For stiffer frosting, add up to ½ cup (63 grams) more confectioners' sugar to the mixture and beat on high to incorporate.

Chocolate chip cookies are perfect vehicles for joy. There is no other cookie loved as much, and if I had to eat one type of cookie for the rest of my life, it would be this one. I tinkered with and tested this recipe over and over—until I arrived at this version, which feels pretty perfect. I love the gooey texture of these cookies, and how the salt contrasts the sweet notes and makes the chocolate and caramel even more pronounced. I talk a lot about self-love and self-worth, and these cookies are just as worthy! You are worthy of them! Walk in your truth and greatness.

my favorite salted caramel chocolate chip cookies

MAKES ABOUT 28 COOKIES

2¾ cups (345 grams) **all-purpose flour**
2 teaspoons **cornstarch**
1 teaspoon **baking powder**
1 teaspoon **baking soda**
1 teaspoon **kosher salt**
1 cup (2 sticks/226 grams) **unsalted butter**, at room temperature

½ cup (100 grams) **granulated sugar**
1½ cups packed (330 grams) **light brown sugar**
1 large **egg**, at room temperature
2 large **egg yolks**, at room temperature
1 tablespoon **vanilla extract**

2 cups (350 grams) **semisweet chocolate chips**
Soft caramels, such as Werther's Original, unwrapped (you'll need about 28)
Flaky sea salt, such as fleur de sel or Maldon

1. Position a rack in the middle of the oven and preheat to 350°F. Line two large rimmed baking sheets with parchment paper.

2. In a medium bowl, whisk together the flour, cornstarch, baking powder, baking soda, and kosher salt.

3. In the bowl of a stand mixer fitted with the paddle attachment, beat the butter and both sugars on high speed until light and fluffy, about 3 minutes. Add the egg and the egg yolks one at a time, making sure each is incorporated before adding the next and stopping to scrape down the sides and bottom

of the bowl between additions. Add the vanilla and beat until incorporated. Reduce the mixer speed to low and add the dry ingredients in three additions, mixing well after each addition until fully incorporated. With the mixer still on low, add the chocolate chips just until combined. Cover the bowl with plastic wrap or a large plate and refrigerate until firm, about 2 hours (or chill the dough for up to 2 days).

4. Using a 1-tablespoon measure or a #40 disher, scoop the dough into balls (each should weigh between 20 and 25 grams). Add a soft caramel to one ball of dough, cover with another ball of dough, and roll them together

to form a larger ball of dough with the caramel hidden inside. Place the cookie on one of the prepared baking sheets and sprinkle the top with flaky salt. Repeat with more dough and caramels, spacing the cookies at least 2½ inches apart on the pan (they will spread quite a bit in the oven); you should be able to fit 6 cookies on the pan.

5. Bake one sheet at a time for about 15 minutes, until chewy. If you prefer your cookies on the crisper side, bake for an additional 2 minutes. (I personally love mine super chewy, but it's your world, boos!) Remove from the oven and transfer the cookies, upside down, to a wire rack. (Because the caramel might be gooey on the bottom, it's best to cool them upside down.) Let cool until warm or at room temperature.

6. While one sheet of cookies is cooling, bake the other sheet. Once the first baking sheet has cooled, portion more cookies onto it and repeat until you are out of cookie dough.

7. Store the cookies in an airtight container at room temperature for up to 5 days. If the cookies get too hard, place a slice of bread in the container with them for 8 hours to soften.

CELEBRATE!
An unexpected snow day; a friend who's feeling down

CELEBRATE!
Valentine's Day;
December holiday
gifting; a reunion of
friends or family

Several years ago, I started making holiday gifts for friends and family, and after a wonderful reaction to my salted caramel chocolate chip cookies (page 214), I decided to expand on the edible-present idea. With these caramels, I wanted them to have a seasonal flavor, and when I stumbled upon blood oranges in my grocery store, I knew I'd found the perfect addition. The result is magical: buttery caramels uplifted with the sunny, bright citrus flavor of the blood oranges. Whoever you gift these caramels to will feel showered with love, no matter the occasion.

blood orange caramels

MAKES 64 (1-INCH) CARAMELS

1 cup (224 grams) **fresh blood orange juice**
Nonstick cooking spray
2 cups (400 grams) **granulated sugar**

1½ cups (360 grams) **heavy cream**
1 cup (340 grams) **light corn syrup**

½ cup (1 stick/113 grams) **unsalted butter**
½ teaspoon **kosher salt**
Flaky sea salt, such as fleur de sel or Maldon, for sprinkling

1. In a wide 4-quart saucepan, bring the orange juice to a boil over medium-high heat. Cook, stirring from time to time, until the juice has reduced to about ½ cup and has the consistency of molasses, 40 to 45 minutes.

2. Meanwhile, line an 8-inch square pan with two long sheets of crisscrossed parchment paper, leaving a generous overhang on all sides, then spray with nonstick cooking spray. Place a wire rack near the stove and set the pan on top. Cut 64 (4-inch) squares of waxed paper.

3. In another 4-quart pot with tall sides, combine the sugar, cream, corn syrup, butter, and kosher salt. Add the reduced orange juice and heat over medium-high heat, stirring, to dissolve the sugar and melt the butter. When the mixture comes to a boil, stop stirring and reduce the heat to medium or medium-low (the caramel will foam and bubble and rise, so

adjust the heat as necessary to prevent it from overflowing). Clip a candy thermometer to the pot and cook until the mixture reaches 252°F; this takes about 45 minutes, so be patient.

4. Remove from the heat and pour the caramel into the prepared pan. Sprinkle with the flaky salt and let sit, uncovered, at room temperature for at least 3 hours and up to overnight. Using the parchment sling, lift the caramel block out of the pan and transfer it to a cutting board. Spray a bench scraper or a very sharp (not serrated) knife with nonstick cooking spray and use it to cut the caramels into 1-inch squares or longer rectangles, then wrap each in waxed paper.

5. The caramels can be stored in an airtight container at room temperature for up to 2 weeks or in the refrigerator for up to 4 weeks, but good luck with that (stop trippin')!

When I've lost loved ones in the past, I've found that once I began to feel less constant grief, I started to remember our moments together fondly and want to honor their memory. When Big Mama passed away suddenly in 2018, I experienced all the stages of grief over and over. It took a couple of years until I really was able to look at old videos and photos, bake her recipes, and feel any semblance of joy just thinking of her. Tea cakes were one of Big Mama's signature recipes. I learned later that Big Mama loved to tinker with the recipe's flavors, and I decided to do the same in her honor. As I made these beautifully pink tea cakes, I could feel her smiling down on me, and it filled me with gratitude for everything she meant to me.

raspberry sugar tea cakes

MAKES ABOUT 22 COOKIES

1 cup (28 grams) **freeze-dried raspberries**

1½ cups (188 grams) **all-purpose flour**

½ teaspoon **kosher salt**

¼ teaspoon **baking soda**

¾ cup (150 grams) **granulated sugar**

½ cup (1 stick/113 grams) **unsalted butter**, at room temperature

1 large **egg**, at room temperature

2 teaspoons **vanilla extract**

1. Using a food processor or high-power blender, process the raspberries into a fine powder. Sift through a fine-mesh sieve into a small bowl (discard the seeds). You should get about ¼ cup.

2. In a medium bowl, whisk together the raspberry powder, flour, salt, and baking soda until combined.

3. In the bowl of a stand mixer fitted with the paddle attachment, beat the sugar and butter, starting on medium-high, until pale and fluffy, about 4 minutes. Stop the mixer, add the egg and vanilla, and beat on medium until well incorporated, about 1 minute. Scrape down the bowl with a spatula and beat again to combine.

4. Reduce the mixer speed to low and add the dry ingredients in three increments, making sure each is fully incorporated before adding the next. Cover the bowl and refrigerate until the dough is firm, 1 to 2 hours, or chill for up to 1 day.

5. When ready to bake, position a rack in the middle of the oven and preheat to 325°F. Line two large rimmed baking sheets with parchment paper.

6. Using a 1-tablespoon measuring spoon, scoop up some dough and roll it into a ball. Using your palms, gently press the ball to flatten a bit and place it on one of the baking sheets. Repeat with the rest of the dough, spacing the cookies about 1½ inches apart.

7. Bake one pan of cookies for about 15 minutes, until golden brown on the edges. Remove from the oven and let cool on the baking sheet for 5 to 10 minutes, then transfer to a wire rack and let cool completely before serving. Repeat with the remaining pan of cookies.

CELEBRATE!
A bake day with
your grandmother;
an afternoon tea, of
course; Valentine's
Day

CELEBRATE!
A sophisticated grown-up bday party; singing karaoke for the first time; learning a new hobby

Tarte tatin is one of my favorites and since it often begins with the convenience of store-bought puff pastry, it's simple to throw together, too. From the classic apple to this bananas Foster version, its adaptable nature is why I depend on tarte tatin for unfussy entertaining. Here warming cinnamon and nutmeg heighten bananas that are tenderized in a brown sugar caramel. With a splash of rum, this dessert is the perfect marriage of NOLA and French vibes, the very definition of Creole influence.

bananas foster tarte tatin

MAKES ONE 9-INCH TART (SERVES 8)

1 sheet **frozen all-butter puff pastry**, defrosted
3 tablespoons (43 grams) **unsalted butter**

½ cup packed (110 grams) **light brown sugar**
⅛ teaspoon **ground cinnamon**
⅛ teaspoon **freshly grated nutmeg**

⅛ teaspoon **kosher salt**
5 large **firm bananas**, peeled and halved lengthwise
2 tablespoons **dark rum**
Vanilla ice cream, for serving

1. Position a rack in the middle of the oven and preheat to 400°F. Line a large rimmed baking sheet with parchment paper.

2. Cut the puff pastry into a round roughly 10 inches wide. Don't be super precious about it—this is a rustic dessert. Transfer the pastry round to the prepared baking sheet. Make a few ½-inch-long slits in the pastry or use a fork to poke it in a few places. Throw that in the fridge while you work on the caramel and bananas.

3. In a 9-inch ovenproof skillet (preferably stainless steel), melt the butter over medium-high heat. Stir in the brown sugar, cinnamon, nutmeg, and salt and cook, swirling the skillet occasionally, until the mixture turns a medium amber color, about 3 minutes. Arrange the bananas in the caramel and cook, without moving them, until they just start to soften around the edges, 90 seconds to 2 minutes. Pour the rum over the bananas and cook until

it evaporates and the caramel thickens slightly, about 2 minutes. Remove from the heat.

4. Arrange the pastry round over the bananas, tucking it into the skillet around the edge—again, it doesn't have to be perfect. Transfer to the oven and bake for about 25 minutes, until the pastry is golden and puffed.

5. Transfer the pan to a wire rack and let cool for 40 minutes to 1 hour. Place a plate wider than the skillet on top and carefully invert the pan and plate together so the tart ends up on the plate. Serve with vanilla ice cream alongside.

note Since we are cutting corners on time, don't cut corners on quality. An all-butter puff pastry will pay dividends. Dufour is definitely a splurge, while Trader Joe's is shockingly affordable—both are excellent quality and the rich flavor will be well worth it. Butter stay winning.

Go, shawty, it's your birthday! Whether you're up in the club dropping it like it's hot or at the crib sipping on wine, you deserve to celebrate to the fullest. I'm the type that goes hard for a bday, celebrating the entire month. And trust me when I say a cake with candles announcing your age isn't always the fix you need. Be a rebel! Shake it up with a cookie that screams "happy birthday" with the balloons, confetti, Hallmark cards, and Roger Rabbit dance moves. Imagine the fudgiest brownie wrapped in a buttery-soft, chewy, colorful-sprinkle-speckled cookie!

brownie-stuffed birthday cookies

MAKES ABOUT 28 COOKIES

CELEBRATE!
Ya birthday, duh (or not!); after a long hard day (milk and cookies, anyone? You deserve it!)

COOKIE DOUGH
2¾ cups (345 grams) **all-purpose flour**
2 teaspoons **cornstarch**
1 teaspoon **baking powder**
1 teaspoon **baking soda**
1 teaspoon **kosher salt**
1 cup (2 sticks/226 grams) **unsalted butter**, at room temperature
½ cup (100 grams) **granulated sugar**
1½ cups packed (330 grams) **light brown sugar**

1 large **egg**, at room temperature
2 large **egg yolks**, at room temperature
1 tablespoon **vanilla extract**
1 cup (175 grams) **semisweet chocolate chips**
1 cup (175 grams) **white chocolate chips**
1 cup (160 grams) **rainbow sprinkles**

BROWNIES
Nonstick cooking spray
⅓ cup (67 grams) **granulated sugar**

¼ cup packed (55 grams) **light brown sugar**
4 tablespoons (½ stick/ 57 grams) **unsalted butter**, melted
1 large **egg**, at room temperature
1½ teaspoons **vegetable oil** or other neutral oil
1 teaspoon **vanilla extract**
⅓ cup (42 grams) **all-purpose flour**
¼ cup (25 grams) **unsweetened cocoa powder**
¼ teaspoon **kosher salt**

1. **Make the cookie dough:** In a medium bowl, whisk together the flour, cornstarch, baking powder, baking soda, and salt.

2. In the bowl of a stand mixer fitted with the paddle attachment, beat the butter and both sugars on medium-high speed until light and fluffy, about 3 minutes. Add the egg and

egg yolks one at a time, making sure each is incorporated before adding the next and stopping to scrape down the sides and bottom of the bowl between additions. Add the vanilla and beat until incorporated.

recipe continues

3. Reduce the mixer speed to low and add the dry ingredients in three additions, mixing well after each addition until fully incorporated. Scrape down the sides and bottom of the bowl and mix on low briefly to reincorporate. With the mixer on low, mix in the semisweet and white chocolate chips and the sprinkles until just combined. Cover the bowl with plastic wrap or a large plate and refrigerate until firm, about 3 hours, and up to 1 day.

4. **Make the brownies:** While the dough is chilling, position a rack in the middle of the oven and preheat to 350°F. Grease an 8 by 4-inch loaf pan with nonstick cooking spray.

5. In a medium bowl, whisk together both sugars and the melted butter until well combined.

6. Add the egg and mix vigorously until it's very well incorporated, at least 2 minutes (this is your workout, boo). Whisk in the oil and vanilla.

7. In another medium bowl, whisk together the flour, cocoa powder, and salt until combined. Add the dry ingredients to the wet ingredients and mix until incorporated. Transfer the batter to the prepared loaf pan.

8. Bake for 20 to 25 minutes, until a toothpick inserted into the center comes out with a few crumbs attached (but not too many). We want it to be done but not overdone, since we will be baking it again. Transfer the pan to a wire rack and let cool completely, then run a small offset spatula or butter knife around the perimeter and turn the brownie block out of the pan. Cut the brownie into ½- to ¾-inch squares. You'll have extra pieces, depending on how small your squares are—you can snack on them. (Name one person that's complained about having extra brownies on hand. I'll wait.)

9. **Make the brownie-stuffed cookies:** Position a rack in the middle of the oven and preheat to 350°F. Line two large rimmed baking sheets with parchment paper.

10. Using a 2-tablespoon cookie scoop or a #30 disher, scoop the dough into balls (each should weigh between 50 and 55 grams). You should end up with between 28 and 30 balls. Flatten one ball of dough into a "pancake" and place a piece of brownie in the center, then wrap the cookie dough around the brownie, encasing it completely (though if you have a brownie bit peeking out here and there, don't panic, boos). Gently roll the dough back into a ball and set it on one of the prepared baking sheets. (Alternatively, use a 1-tablespoon measuring spoon to form balls of dough that weigh 25 or so grams each. Press two balls of dough into "pancakes," then place a brownie piece in the center of one pancake, cover it with the other, and gently roll them together into a larger ball with the brownie hidden inside, then set on the pan.) Repeat with the remaining dough balls and brownie pieces, spacing the cookies at least 2½ inches apart on the baking sheets; you should fit 6 cookies on each pan.

11. Put one pan of cookies in the refrigerator. (You can also freeze whatever cookies you don't want to bake right away on the baking sheet, then transfer them to a zip-top bag and store them in the freezer.) Bake the other pan of cookies for about 16 minutes, until spread out and golden around the edges. If you prefer your cookies on the crispier side, bake for an additional 2 minutes. Remove from the oven and immediately transfer to a wire rack to cool until warm, or let cool completely before serving. Repeat to bake the remaining cookies.

12. Store in an airtight container at room temperature for up to 5 days. If the cookies get too hard, place a slice of bread in the container with them and let stand overnight to soften.

note If you're baking cookies from frozen, add a couple of minutes to the baking time. If you're freezing your balls of cookie dough for more than a couple of weeks, wrap them in another freezer bag to prevent freezer burn.

Even in a book about celebration and cultivating joy, we need a real-talk moment. Sometimes in life, we just ain't feeling it. We've done our affirmations, we smiled our fake-ass smiles in hopes of developing them into authentic ones, and we even wrote in our gratitude journals. But sometimes things just don't click. The glass doesn't feel half-full. And guess what? That's okay. Lean into that moment, and if it means you need a good cry, cry your heart out! If it means you need a day in complete solitude, eating your feelings with a dozen of these gooey, decadent shortbread bars, so be it. Sometimes we need a reset to return to joy. And if an entire pan of these bars goes missing in the process, at least you had a delicious time in the midst of the valley.

chocolate pecan pie shortbread bars

MAKES 12 BARS

SHORTBREAD CRUST

1½ cups (3 sticks/340 grams) **unsalted butter**, at room temperature

1 cup (200 grams) **granulated sugar**

1 teaspoon **kosher salt**

1 large **egg**, lightly beaten

2 teaspoons **vanilla extract**

3½ cups (438 grams) **all-purpose flour**, plus more for dusting

PECAN TOPPING

1½ cups (192 grams) **pecan halves**

1 cup (320 grams) **sorghum molasses** or maple syrup

½ cup packed (110 grams) **light brown sugar**

½ cup (100 grams) **granulated sugar**

½ cup (1 stick/113 grams) **unsalted butter**

4 large **eggs**, at room temperature

¼ cup (56 grams) **bourbon**

2 teaspoons **vanilla extract**

1 teaspoon **kosher salt**

½ teaspoon **ground cinnamon**

¼ teaspoon **ground ginger**

½ cup (85 grams) **semisweet chocolate chips**

Whipped cream or vanilla ice cream, for serving (optional, but highly recommended)

1. **Make the shortbread crust:** Position a rack in the middle of the oven and preheat to 350°F. Line a 9 by 13-inch baking pan with parchment paper, leaving a generous amount overhanging the longer sides.

2. In the bowl of a stand mixer fitted with the paddle attachment or in a large bowl using a handheld mixer, beat together the butter, granulated sugar, and salt on medium speed until light and fluffy, about 2 minutes. Add

recipe continues

the egg and vanilla and beat on medium to incorporate. Scrape down the sides and bottom of the bowl to ensure everything is incorporated and briefly beat again to recombine. Add the flour in two increments, mixing on medium speed until just combined and the dough just comes together.

3. Transfer the dough to the prepared baking pan. Lightly dust your fingers and palms with flour and gently press the dough into the pan. Score the dough all over with the tines of a fork. Bake for 40 to 45 minutes, until baked through and golden. Transfer the pan to a wire rack (keep the oven on) and let cool.

4. **Make the pecan topping:** Spread the pecans over a small rimmed baking sheet in a single layer and toast in the oven for 10 minutes, or until fragrant, tossing halfway through. Transfer the pecans to a bowl and let them chillax while you finish up the topping; keep the oven on.

5. In a small saucepan, combine the sorghum molasses, both sugars, and the butter and cook over medium heat, stirring occasionally, until the butter melts, the sugars dissolve, and the mixture is combined, about 6 minutes. Remove from the heat, pour into a medium bowl, and let cool.

6. In another medium bowl, whisk together the eggs, bourbon, vanilla, salt, cinnamon, and ginger until combined.

7. When the syrup mixture is cool enough to touch, whisk in the egg mixture until combined. Add the pecans and chocolate chips and stir until combined. Pour the filling over the shortbread crust and, using a small offset spatula or butter knife, evenly spread it out.

8. Bake for 30 to 35 minutes, until the liquid no longer jiggles if you shake the pan. Let the bars set at room temperature for about 30 minutes, then pop in the fridge until pretty set, about 1 hour. You're looking for a pecan-pie-filling consistency.

9. When ready to serve, cut twelve 3¼ by 2½-inch bars and dig in. These are beyond bomb with some whipped cream—just sayin'. And if you really want to live dangerously, warm up a piece to enjoy with a scoop of vanilla ice cream.

CELEBRATE!
A not-so-sunny day; Thanksgiving (for a unique treat that's not quite pie)

When I was little, I was obsessed with strawberry ice cream, specifically the Very Berry Strawberry at Baskin-Robbins. My mom and dad treated me to weekly scoops, and I even went through a phase when I would want nothing but ice cream cakes for my birthday. It wasn't surprising that my daughter, Harmony, loves strawberries just as much. That's my baby! So, of course, I had to make a strawberry ice cream just for her. You may notice that in addition to the egg yolks, I also use whole eggs. The egg whites give the ice cream lightness, while the yolks help with a smooth mouthfeel. If you can get your hands on peak-season local strawberries, definitely give this ice cream a whirl.

harmony's favorite strawberry ice cream

MAKES 2 QUARTS

1 pound (454 grams) **strawberries**, hulled

1½ cups plus 2 tablespoons (325 grams) **granulated sugar**, divided

¾ teaspoon **kosher salt**

3 large **eggs**

2 large **egg yolks**

2 cups (480 grams) **heavy cream**

2 cups (480 grams) **half-and-half**

1 tablespoon **vanilla extract**

1. In a food processor, combine the strawberries, 2 tablespoons of the sugar, and salt and process until smooth. Slide to the side.

2. In a large bowl, whisk together the eggs and egg yolks until combined. Whisk in the remaining 1½ cups sugar until fully combined.

3. In a medium pot, combine the heavy cream and half-and-half and heat over medium heat, stirring often to prevent scorching on the bottom, just until steam starts to rise off the surface. Remove from the heat.

4. Place a folded kitchen towel on the counter and set the bowl with the egg-sugar mixture on top (this prevents the bowl from doing the Electric Slide). While whisking continuously, use a small ladle to slowly drizzle about 3 tablespoons of the hot dairy mixture into the egg mixture to temper it. Still whisking continuously, slowly drizzle in the rest of the dairy mixture, then stir in strawberry puree and vanilla to incorporate. Transfer the custard to a 2-quart container, cover, and refrigerate until completely cold, at least 6 hours or preferably overnight.

5. Transfer half the chilled custard to the ice cream maker (leave the rest in the fridge) and churn according to the manufacturer's instructions. Transfer to a container and freeze for at least 4 hours, or until firm, before serving. Repeat to churn the remaining custard. Scoop it up and get at it!

CELEBRATE!
Strawberry picking; any summer day; National Eat Ice Cream for Breakfast Day on February 6

Nothing says "love" like a whole mess of plump beignets suffocated in a heavy blanket of snowy powdered sugar. In fact, beignets should be considered the sixth love language. I devour them with a big ol' smile on my face every time. These plantain beignets brought that same smile to my face while I was developing the recipe. And while I've taken a bit of liberty with the term "beignet," since these aren't yeasted, they do have a thick, leavened-dough coating that puffs in the same way as traditional beignets do once fried. Just as with the original, I smother these beignets in powdered sugar and drizzle on a coconut-rum sauce that nods to the Caribbean.

plantain beignets with coconut–rum sauce

MAKES 20 TO 22 BEIGNETS

COCONUT-RUM SAUCE
1 cup **full-fat coconut milk**
3 tablespoons **granulated sugar**
2 tablespoons (28 grams) **unsalted butter**
2 teaspoons **dark rum**
¼ teaspoon **vanilla extract**
¼ teaspoon **ground cinnamon**
Pinch of **freshly grated nutmeg**
Pinch of **fine sea salt**

PLANTAINS
4 tablespoons (½ stick/ 57 grams) cold **unsalted butter**, divided
2 very ripe large **plantains** (should be pretty black), sliced 1 inch thick

BEIGNETS
3 cups **vegetable oil**
1¼ cups (156 grams) **all-purpose flour**, divided
1 tablespoon **granulated sugar**
2 teaspoons **baking powder**
½ teaspoon **fine sea salt**
1 teaspoon **unsalted butter**, melted
1 large **egg**, at room temperature, beaten
¾ cup (168 grams) **whole milk**
½ teaspoon **vanilla extract**
Confectioners' sugar, for dusting

1. **Make the coconut-rum sauce:** In a small saucepan, combine the coconut milk, granulated sugar, and butter. Heat over medium heat until the butter melts, then cook, stirring occasionally, until the sauce has thickened and reduced by about half, 6 to 8 minutes. Add the rum and cook, stirring continuously, for about 1 minute, then whisk in the vanilla, cinnamon, nutmeg, and salt. The finished sauce should be a beautiful, darkened caramel color. Remove from the heat and keep warm.

recipe continues

2. **Cook the plantains:** Heat a large skillet over medium heat until hot enough that you can hold your hand over it for only a few seconds, then melt 2 tablespoons of the butter. Working in batches, arrange the plantains in the pan in a single layer, leaving some space between the slices. Cook until golden on the bottom, about 3 minutes, then gently flip and cook until golden on the other side, about 2 minutes more. Transfer the plantains to a paper towel–lined plate and repeat with the remaining butter and plantains. Let cool while you start beigneting!

3. **Make the beignets:** In a medium pot, heat the oil over medium-high heat until it registers between 350° and 375°F on an instant-read thermometer. Set a wire rack over a large rimmed baking sheet.

4. Sift 1 cup (125 grams) of the flour into a medium bowl and add the granulated sugar, baking powder, and salt. Add the melted butter, egg, milk, and vanilla extract to the dry ingredients and stir until a smooth, thick batter forms.

5. Put the remaining ¼ cup (31 grams) flour in a shallow bowl. Roll the plantain pieces in the flour, then shake off the excess (the flour helps the batter adhere) and dip them into the batter.

6. Gently slide the beignets into the hot oil and fry until golden brown, turning gently from time to time, about 2 minutes. Adjust the heat as necessary to maintain the oil temperature. Transfer to the prepared rack and immediately dust with confectioners' sugar.

7. Serve the beignets hot or warm, with the coconut-rum sauce on the side for dipping.

CELEBRATE!
Dessert in bed; moving in together (like I said, the ultimate love language)

At an early point in my *Grandbaby Cakes* journey, my followers started dubbing me the "Queen of Pound Cakes." I graciously accepted this title and now refer to myself this way in all settings, from random conversations with strangers to professional Zoom meetings. I slightly kid—the point is, I am honored by the appointment and have taken it seriously. The first cake I ever learned to bake was my mama's pound cake; I was still a child and aimed at perfecting it. Since then, I've been coming up with unique flavor combinations and textures, and *Grandbaby Cakes* has become a hub for numerous pound cakes, all completely different and all to die for. The trick to pound cake success rests in nailing the moistness and texture; bonus points for creative flavors. And that's where this cake shines! A moist, tender, sweet potato pound cake, filled with a crisp pecan coffee cake swirl and finished with a silky Nawlins-inspired praline glaze takes creativity and taste to new heights. The queen has spoken.

praline sweet potato pound cake

MAKES ONE 10-CUP BUNDT CAKE (SERVES 10 TO 12)

PRALINE SWIRL
⅔ cup packed (145 grams) **light brown sugar**
⅓ cup (40 grams) finely chopped **pecans**
5 tablespoons (71 grams) **unsalted butter**, melted
2 tablespoons **all-purpose flour**
1½ teaspoons **ground cinnamon**
1 teaspoon **vanilla extract**

> **CELEBRATE!**
> First day of fall; welcoming new neighbors; switching back to hot coffee after a summer of cold brew

CAKE
1 cup (2 sticks/226 grams) **unsalted butter**, at room temperature, plus more for greasing the pan
3 cups (375 grams) **all-purpose flour**, sifted, plus more for dusting the pan
1½ teaspoons **baking powder**
1 teaspoon **ground cinnamon**
1 teaspoon **kosher salt**
½ teaspoon **baking soda**
¼ teaspoon **freshly grated nutmeg**
2 cups (400 grams) **granulated sugar**
5 large **eggs**, at room temperature
¾ cup (170 grams) **sour cream**, at room temperature
¾ cup (170 grams) mashed **sweet potato**
1½ tablespoons **vanilla extract**

PRALINE GLAZE
5 tablespoons (71 grams) **unsalted butter**
½ cup packed (110 grams) **light brown sugar**
½ cup **heavy cream**
1 tablespoon **light corn syrup**
½ teaspoon **vanilla extract**
½ teaspoon **kosher salt**
1½ cups (150 grams) chopped **pecans**

recipe continues

1. **Make the praline swirl:** In a medium bowl, whisk together the brown sugar, pecans, butter, flour, cinnamon, and vanilla until thoroughly combined. Throw that in the fridge while you make the cake.

2. **Make the cake:** Position a rack in the middle of the oven and preheat to 350°F. Liberally grease a 10-cup Bundt pan with butter and dust with flour.

3. In a medium bowl, whisk together the flour, baking powder, cinnamon, salt, baking soda, and nutmeg until well combined.

4. In the bowl of a stand mixer fitted with the paddle attachment, beat together the butter and granulated sugar on high speed until light and fluffy, about 5 minutes. Add the eggs one at a time, ensuring that each egg is incorporated before adding the next. You may want to stop the mixer after each addition and scrape down the sides and bottom of the bowl with a spatula to ensure everything is well incorporated. Add the sour cream, sweet potato, and vanilla and beat on medium speed until incorporated (the batter will look curdled, but no worries—it's all good). Reduce the mixer speed to low, carefully add the dry ingredients to the wet ingredients, and mix until just combined; the batter will be thick.

5. Scoop half the batter into the prepared Bundt pan. Remove the praline swirl mixture from the refrigerator and break it up into crumbles with a fork, then sprinkle the mixture over the batter in the pan. Scoop the remaining batter into the pan and, using a small offset spatula, smooth out the top. Bake for 50 to 60 minutes, until a toothpick inserted into the center comes out moist but mostly clean. Transfer to a wire rack and let cool in the pan for 10 minutes, then invert the cake onto the rack and let cool completely before glazing.

6. **Make the praline glaze:** In a medium saucepan, combine the butter, brown sugar, heavy cream, corn syrup, vanilla, and salt and cook over medium heat, stirring frequently, until the mixture comes to a simmer. Stir in the pecans until completely coated and remove from the heat. Transfer the glaze to a liquid measuring cup and let cool completely before using.

7. Pour the glaze over the cooled cake and let set for about 25 minutes before slicing and serving it up.

A cheesecake inspired by Prince? I'm down. Ya see, my connection to Prince goes beyond general fandom—we also happen to share a birthday, June 7. I've always loved how he danced to the beat of his own drum and stood in his truth (in heels, of course). What truly makes each of us great is our ability to be ourselves and celebrate our unique ways—the more offbeat, the better! Let's go crazy! Let's get nuts! This cheesecake, with its distinctive lilac hue from purple sweet potato and swirls of vanilla batter, all but dances on your plate. Its rich and creamy texture shows up and shows out, deserving of a mic-drop moment. It's the kind of showstopping entrance Prince would have been proud of.

purple rain sweet potato swirl cheesecake

MAKES ONE 10-INCH CHEESECAKE (SERVES 12)

CRUST
Nonstick baking spray
1½ cups (245 grams) gingersnap crumbs (from 28 gingersnaps, ground to crumbs in a food processor)
3 tablespoons granulated sugar
5 tablespoons (70 grams) salted butter, melted

FILLING
3 (8-ounce/225-gram) packages Philadelphia cream cheese, at room temperature
1¼ cups (250 grams) granulated sugar
½ cup (120 grams) heavy cream, at room temperature
3 large eggs, at room temperature
¾ cup (169 grams) sour cream, at room temperature
2 tablespoons all-purpose flour
2 teaspoons vanilla extract
¾ cup (170 grams) mashed purple sweet potato (from about 1 potato; can substitute with regular sweet potato, but then omit the dark brown sugar)
1 tablespoon packed dark brown sugar
1 teaspoon ground cinnamon
⅛ teaspoon freshly grated nutmeg
⅛ teaspoon ground ginger

1. **Make the crust:** Position a rack in the middle of the oven and preheat to 350°F. Spray the bottom and sides of a 10-inch springform pan with at least 2¾-inch-tall sides with nonstick baking spray.

2. In a large bowl, stir together the gingersnap crumbs and granulated sugar until combined. Pour in the melted butter and stir until the mixture is the consistency of wet sand. Press the mixture over the bottom of the greased

recipe continues

pan and bake for about 10 minutes, until nice and golden. Transfer to a wire rack to cool while you prepare the filling; keep the oven on.

3. **Make the filling:** In the bowl of a stand mixer fitted with the paddle or whisk attachment, or in a large bowl using a handheld mixer, beat the cream cheese and granulated sugar on medium-high speed until smooth, about 2 minutes. Beat in the heavy cream until combined, then add the eggs one at a time, beating until incorporated after each addition. Stop the mixer and scrape down the sides and bottom of the bowl, then briefly mix on medium-high speed to incorporate. Add the sour cream, flour, and vanilla and mix on medium-high until smooth. Scoop out about 2 cups of the cheesecake mixture and set aside.

4. Add the sweet potato, brown sugar, cinnamon, nutmeg, and ginger to the remaining mixture and beat on medium-high speed until smooth. The filling may have flecks of sweet potato throughout—it's all good if it does.

CELEBRATE!
A rainy-day project; checking off a big dream; another manic Monday (see what I did there?)

5. Scoop about half (2 cups) of the sweet potato mixture over the cooled crust, then use a small offset spatula to spread it into an even layer. Dollop about 1½ cups of the plain filling on top. Using a butter knife or skewer, gently, as not to scrape the crust, make swirls in the batter—you want to see the vivid purple and creamy white batters distinctively in your design, so don't overdo it. Pour the remaining sweet potato filling on top, spreading it evenly, and gently dot with the remaining plain filling. Carefully add decorative swirls to the top.

6. Bake for about 50 minutes, until the center is still a tiny bit jiggly but almost set. (If you want to guarantee no cracks in the cheesecake, wrap the bottom of the pan in aluminum foil [make sure it is completely covered so the cheesecake doesn't get soggy] and place it in a large roasting pan. Add enough hot water to come halfway up the sides of the springform pan and bake as instructed above.) Turn the oven off and open the door just slightly; let the cheesecake cool in the oven for 2 hours. Remove from the oven and let cool completely, about 1 hour, then cover and refrigerate for at least 7 to 8 hours before serving (why does cheesecake take so dang long to make?).

Ah, fall, my favorite season. The changing leaves, brisk mornings, pies for the holiday season (or just because), and, yes, apple picking, a tradition I adopted from my in-laws. Every year at the onset of autumn, we visit places like the County Line Orchard in Indiana. From music in the barnyard to the kids' petting zoo Harmony adored, we all fell in love with the place. Each time, I leave with plenty of apple cider, apple cinnamon donuts, and, duh, apples. But instead of spending all day making pie, I opted for a moist, spiced snacking cake. You'll have the rest of the season to bake pies, so take it easy and have a slice of this cake with your morning coffee—or whenever you need a pick-me-up.

salted butterscotch apple whiskey snacking cake
MAKES ONE 9-INCH ROUND CAKE (SERVES 8 TO 10)

CAKE
Nonstick baking spray
1½ cups (188 grams) **all-purpose flour**
¾ cup packed (170 grams) **light brown sugar**
2 teaspoons **ground cinnamon**
1½ teaspoons **baking powder**
½ teaspoon **baking soda**
½ teaspoon **fine sea salt**
½ teaspoon **freshly grated nutmeg**
½ teaspoon **ground ginger**
½ cup (105 grams) **vegetable oil**

⅓ cup (75 grams) **sour cream**
¼ cup (63 grams) **applesauce**
2 large **eggs**, at room temperature
2 tablespoons **whiskey**
1½ teaspoons **vanilla extract**
1 large **apple** (250 grams), peeled, cored, and cut into ¾-inch dice (about 2 cups)

ICING
3 tablespoons (42 grams) **unsalted butter**
⅓ cup packed (75 grams) **dark brown sugar**

1½ teaspoons **hot water**
2 tablespoons **heavy cream**, plus more as needed
1 tablespoon **whiskey**
½ teaspoon **vanilla extract**
⅛ teaspoon **fine sea salt**, plus more to taste and for sprinkling on top
½ cup plus 2 tablespoons (62 grams) sifted **confectioners' sugar**
Flaky sea salt, such as fleur de sel or Maldon, for serving

1. **Make the cake:** Position a rack in the middle of the oven and preheat to 350°F. Spray a 9-inch round cake pan with nonstick baking spray and line the bottom with parchment paper cut to fit, then spray the parchment.

2. In a large bowl, whisk together the flour, light brown sugar, cinnamon, baking powder, baking soda, fine sea salt, nutmeg, and ginger until combined.

recipe continues

3. In a small bowl or measuring cup, whisk together the oil, sour cream, applesauce, eggs, whiskey, and vanilla until thoroughly combined. Add the wet ingredients to the dry ingredients and, using a flexible spatula, stir just until a smooth and uniform batter forms. Gently fold in the apples; we don't wanna overmix.

4. Transfer the batter to the prepared pan and bake for 35 to 40 minutes, until the cake is golden brown and a toothpick inserted into the center comes out clean. Transfer the pan to a wire rack and let cool for 5 minutes. Turn the cake out onto the rack and let cool completely.

5. Make the icing: While the cake is cooling, in a heavy-bottomed small saucepan with tall sides, melt the butter over low to medium-low heat, then cook until the solids turn medium-brown and the butter smells nutty, 5 to 6 minutes. Add the dark brown sugar and hot water and stir to moisten all the sugar. Cook until the brown sugar has liquefied and the mixture is darker and bubbling vigorously, about 5 minutes. During this time, stir the mixture well, scraping the corners of the pan to incorporate any remaining brown sugar.

6. Stir in the cream; you may wanna step back because the mixture will bubble up. Cook until the mixture turns smooth and glossy, 3 to 4 minutes more, then stir in the whiskey and vanilla and cook until the alcohol cooks off, about 2 minutes. Remove from the heat and stir in the sea salt. Taste and season with more fine sea salt, if ya need. Let cool for about 5 minutes; the butterscotch will continue to thicken as it cools. You should have a scant 1 cup butterscotch.

7. Whisk the confectioners' sugar into the cooled butterscotch until fully incorporated. Add more cream, 1 to 2 teaspoons at a time, until you reach spreadable consistency. If it gets too thin, add a bit more confectioners' sugar. Using a small offset spatula, spread the icing over the cake, sprinkle with flaky sea salt, then slice and enjoy!

CELEBRATE!
A day of apple picking; Fall Back (end of Daylight Saving gains an extra hour, boos!)

When Big Mama passed away, I was blessed to inherit her cookbooks. While leafing through her recipes, I came upon one for angel pie, stained and splattered all over—clearly a dessert she had made, and loved, a lot. For those unfamiliar with it, lemon angel pie is a vintage Southern recipe that hasn't gotten a lot of love. It looks like a reversed lemon meringue pie, where a baked meringue shell is filled with lemon curd and then topped with whipped cream. Think of a Pavlova, but with a pielike structure.

I decided to pay homage to this beautiful dessert with my own twist: I added finely ground freeze-dried strawberries to evoke that iconic summer thirst-quencher, strawberry lemonade. Whenever I make it, I like to imagine Big Mama is right there with me, looking over my shoulder—she would have loved this twist.

strawberry lemonade angel pie

MAKES ONE 9-INCH PIE (SERVES 6 TO 8)

MERINGUE SHELL
Nonstick cooking spray
¾ cup (16 grams) **freeze-dried strawberries**
4 large **egg whites**, at room temperature
½ teaspoon **cream of tartar**
Pinch of **fine sea salt**
1 cup (200 grams) **granulated sugar**

LEMON FILLING AND WHIPPED CREAM
4 large **egg yolks**, at room temperature
1 (14-ounce/396-gram) can **sweetened condensed milk**
2 teaspoons finely grated **lemon zest** (from 1 lemon)
½ cup (112 grams) **fresh lemon juice** (from 2 lemons)
1 teaspoon **vanilla extract**
1 cup (240 grams) cold **heavy cream**

MACERATED STRAWBERRIES AND TOPPING
1 pound (454 grams) **strawberries**, hulled and sliced
¼ cup (50 grams) **granulated sugar**
Finely grated **zest and juice** of 1 small lemon, plus more for garnish

1. Make the meringue shell: Position a rack in the middle of the oven and preheat to 300°F. Spray a 9-inch pie plate with cooking spray.

2. In a mini food processor, pulse the freeze-dried strawberries until ground to a fine dust. Pass the ground strawberries through a fine-mesh sieve and discard the seeds. Set the powdered strawberries aside; you should have about 3 tablespoons.

recipe continues

3. In the bowl of a stand mixer fitted with the whisk attachment or in a large bowl using a handheld mixer, beat the eggs whites on high speed until foamy, about 1 minute. Sprinkle in the cream of tartar and salt and beat until the whites hold soft peaks, about 2 minutes. Gradually add the sugar and beat until the meringue is glossy and stiff, about 2 minutes. Add the powdered strawberries and beat on high until fully incorporated and the meringue is pale pink.

4. Transfer the meringue to the prepared pie plate and, using a small offset spatula, spread it over the bottom and up the sides of the plate to resemble a pie shell. Bake for about 50 minutes, until the meringue is baked through and lightly browned around the sides. Transfer the pie plate to a wire rack and let cool completely. Raise the oven temperature to 350°F. The meringue shell will look somewhat puffed up, as if it won't fit the filling, but just chill. It will deflate as it cools.

5. Make the lemon filling and whipped cream: In a medium bowl, whisk together the egg yolks, sweetened condensed milk, and lemon zest. Gradually whisk in the lemon juice and vanilla until fully combined.

6. Pour the filling into the cooled meringue shell and bake for 20 minutes, or until the filling is mostly set but still jiggles slightly if you shake the pie plate. Transfer to a wire rack and let cool completely.

7. In a chilled large bowl using a handheld mixer, beat the heavy cream, starting on medium speed and increasing to high, until stiff peaks form, about 2 minutes.

8. Top the pie with the whipped cream, making decorative swirls with an offset spatula. Transfer to the fridge and chill for at least 6 hours and up to overnight.

9. Macerate the strawberries: About 1 hour before serving, in a medium bowl, gently stir together the strawberries, sugar, and lemon zest (reserving some zest for garnish) and juice until combined. Cover and let sit at room temperature until ready to serve.

10. Remove the pie from the refrigerator, slice, and serve it up with the macerated strawberries and extra lemon zest on top.

CELEBRATE!
End of school year; getting into college; peak-season strawberries at the greenmarket

Peach cobbler is my family's signature dessert, and Big Mama, whose cobbler was the best, inspired me to master it. She had always topped hers with a piecrust, which may be a Southern tradition. When folk unfamiliar with Southern cooking see my cobbler, they always go, "Is that a big pie?" No, honey, it's a cobbler! A cobbler is messy and syrupy, juices running everywhere—you gotta scoop the heck out of that thing—whereas a pie is more set up. Here I kept the bones of Big Mama's recipe, but added a buttered Baileys sauce to highlight the silky texture of the peaches.

This recipe works with fresh, frozen, or canned peaches. My default is accessible and affordable canned—Big Mama used to put up her own, but store-bought is fine, boos. This way, you can enjoy peach cobbler even on Thanksgiving.

tipsy buttered baileys peach cobbler

SERVES 10 TO 12

FILLING

6 (15-ounce/425-gram) cans **peaches** in very lite syrup or 12 cups sliced peeled fresh or frozen peaches (see Note)
½ cup (1 stick/113 grams) **unsalted butter**
1 cup (200 grams) **granulated sugar**
1 tablespoon **vanilla extract**
1½ teaspoons **freshly grated nutmeg**
½ teaspoon **ground cinnamon**
½ teaspoon **kosher salt**
1 tablespoon **all-purpose flour**

CRUST

2½ cups (315 grams) **all-purpose flour**, plus more for dusting
2 teaspoons **granulated sugar**
1 teaspoon **kosher salt**
1 cup (2 sticks/226 grams) very cold **unsalted butter**, cubed
½ cup (112 grams) **ice water**
1 large **egg**, at room temperature
Demerara sugar, for sprinkling
Ground cinnamon, for dusting

BUTTERED BAILEYS SAUCE

½ cup (1 stick/113 grams) **unsalted butter**
½ cup (100 grams) **granulated sugar**
½ cup (120 grams) **Baileys Irish cream**
2 teaspoons **all-purpose flour**
1 teaspoon **vanilla extract**
¼ teaspoon **kosher salt**

Vanilla ice cream, for serving

1. Make the filling: Drain 4 cans of peaches and transfer to a large pot. Add the remaining peaches with their syrup and the butter. Cook over medium heat, stirring, until the butter melts and combines with the peaches and sauce, about 8 minutes. Stir in the granulated

recipe continues

sugar, vanilla, nutmeg, cinnamon, and salt and bring to a boil. Transfer 3 tablespoons of peach syrup to a small bowl, whisk in the flour, and return it to the pot, whisking to incorporate.

2. Cook, stirring occasionally, until the syrup thickens and coats the back of a spoon, about 30 minutes. Adjust the heat as necessary to maintain a lively simmer. Remove from the heat and let cool completely; the syrup will continue to thicken. (You can refrigerate the filling for up to 2 days.)

3. **Make the crust:** In a large bowl, whisk together the flour, granulated sugar, and salt until combined. Add the butter and, using a pastry cutter, cut it into the flour mixture until the butter pieces range from lima bean to pea size. (You can also squish the butter into flat flakes using your fingers, tossing the butter in the flour with your hands. Put the kids to work on this!) Drizzle the ice water into the mixture 1 tablespoon at a time, until a rough, shaggy dough forms (you will need between 6 and 8 tablespoons water, possibly more). Quickly knead the dough to bring it together—don't worry if there is flour left in the bowl or if the dough isn't totally uniform (once the dough hydrates and rests, it will come more together).

4. Transfer the dough to the counter or board, divide it in half, and shape each into a 3 by 5-inch rectangle. Wrap each rectangle tightly in plastic wrap and refrigerate for at least 1 hour and up to 2 days. (You can also make the dough ahead and freeze it, tightly wrapped in several layers of plastic wrap, for up to 2 months.)

5. **To assemble:** Position a rack in the middle of the oven and preheat to 375°F.

6. Lightly flour a work surface. Unwrap one rectangle of dough and place it on the floured surface. Let the dough sit for about 5 minutes, then, working quickly, roll the dough out to a

roughly 9 by 13-inch rectangle a little less than ¼-inch-thick. Every few rolls, turn the dough a quarter turn, and reflour the counter as necessary to prevent the dough from sticking. You may want to flip the dough and continue to roll. When dusting the dough with flour, err on using less—just enough so the dough isn't sticky. Fit the dough over the bottom of a 9 by 13 by 2-inch baking pan and press the sides up slightly so they come up a smidge.

7. Using a slotted spoon, scoop the peaches over the dough, then pour that glorious syrup on top. Roll out the remaining dough and use it to decorate the top how you see fit. You can do a plain crust or a lattice or cut out various fun shapes.

8. In a small bowl, whisk together the egg and 1 teaspoon water. Brush the top crust with the egg wash, then sprinkle lightly with Demerara sugar and cinnamon. Bake for about 50 minutes, until the crust is golden brown. (If using refrigerated filling, increase the baking time to 60 to 70 minutes.) Transfer to a wire rack and let cool while you make the sauce.

9. **While the cobbler is cooling, let's get saucy!** In a medium saucepan, melt the butter over medium heat. Whisk in the granulated sugar and Baileys and bring the mixture to a boil. Cook until slightly thickened, 2 to 3 minutes, then remove from the heat and whisk in the flour, vanilla, and salt until combined.

10. Serve the cobbler with the sauce for drizzling over and vanilla ice cream on the side.

note If using fresh or frozen sliced peaches, you will have about 12 cups total, versus about 9 cups if using canned peaches. This is because raw peaches occupy more volume. Since you won't have the syrup, toss in another stick (113 grams) of butter to make up for the liquid (more butter equals more fun, anyway!).

CELEBRATE!
Getting 8 hours of sleep for an entire week! Peach season; planting your first garden

"Hon, are ya hungry?" was the customary greeting of Aunt Henrietta, Big Mama's older sister. Protecting her private domain, aka the kitchen, she always fixed you a plate, watched you devour each bite, then she'd see you right out. (She loved basketball and couldn't wait to enjoy her fave Chicago Bulls, so ya had to go!) These butter rolls were one of Aunt Hen's specialties. She would expertly roll out the dough until almost paper thin and meticulously smear butter across the surface, then make it rain sugar and nutmeg on top. After rolling the dough into a log, Aunt Hen would cut it like cinnamon rolls, then drench the rolls in a sublime sauce made with sweet, thickened milk. The result was tender, spiced, syrupy, delightful, and unique—just like Aunt Hen herself.

aunt hen's ol'-school butter rolls

MAKES 24 ROLLS

DOUGH
2 cups (260 grams) **self-rising flour**, plus more for dusting
½ cup (1 stick/113 grams) cold **unsalted butter**, cut into cubes
½ cup (112 grams) **ice water**

FILLING
½ cup (1 stick/113 grams) **unsalted butter**, at room temperature
⅓ cup (67 grams) **granulated sugar**
½ teaspoon **freshly grated nutmeg**
½ teaspoon **ground cinnamon**

SAUCE
2 cups (448 grams) **whole milk**
⅔ cup (132 grams) **granulated sugar**
3 tablespoons (42 grams) **unsalted butter**
¼ teaspoon **kosher salt**
2 teaspoons **vanilla extract**

1. **Make the dough:** In a food processor, combine the flour and the butter and pulse until pea-size crumbs begin to form. Drizzle in the ice water while continuing to pulse until a loose dough forms.

2. Lightly flour your work surface and transfer the dough to it. Cut it in half, then shape each half into a flat rectangular shape. Take the first rectangle (put the other in the fridge) and, using a lightly floured rolling pin, roll the dough out to a roughly 12 by 17-inch rectangle. If the dough starts to tear, don't roll it out any further.

3. **Make the filling:** Spread half (57 grams) of the softened butter all over the dough. In a small bowl, whisk together the sugar, nutmeg, and cinnamon, then sprinkle the buttered dough with half of the sugar mixture. Carefully and very tightly, starting on the long side roll the dough into a log as if making cinnamon rolls. Pinch the seam a bit just to seal in that

filling. Cut the dough crosswise into 12 equal pieces: First cut it in half, then cut each half in half, then cut each of those pieces into thirds. Repeat with the remaining dough, butter, and spices to make 24 rolls total.

4. Make the sauce: In a medium saucepan, combine the milk, sugar, butter, and salt and bring to a boil over medium heat, stirring from time to time. Remove from the heat and stir in the vanilla.

5. Arrange the rolls cut-side up in a large, wide Dutch oven or large pot, then pour the milk sauce over the top. Turn the heat to medium-low and let the rolls puff and cook in the simmering liquid for 30 to 40 minutes, continuing to baste the tops with the milk. These won't brown, but the texture will be gooey AF versus that of the baked rolls. Serve warm from the pot.

VARIATION

Aunt Hen's method is to cook these butter rolls on the stovetop, but if you want them to be really browned and prefer to bake them, here's how you do it: Position a rack in the middle of the oven and preheat to 350°F. Lightly grease a 9 by 13-inch baking pan with butter, then arrange the rolls in the pan cut-side up, as you would for cinnamon rolls. Pour about three-quarters of the milk sauce over the top and reserve the rest.

Bake, basting the rolls a few times with the reserved milk sauce, for 35 to 40 minutes, until the tops turn golden brown and the sauce starts to thicken and bubble. Transfer to a wire rack, let cool for 10 to 15 minutes, then serve warm with the sauce from the pan.

menu suggestions

Juneteenth

Moroccan Ribs with BBQ Date Glaze (page 177)

Peri-Peri Ginger Beer Chicken (page 200)

Georgia Peach Salad with Candied Pecans and Cornbread Croutons (page 86)

Elote Fried Corn Pudding (page 116)

Harmony's Favorite Strawberry Ice Cream (page 228)

Family Fish Fry

Fried Catfish (page 158)

Nashville Hot-Style Catfish (page 159)

Crabby Hush Puppies (page 71)

Watermelon Salad with Tomato, Pickled Onion, Mint, and Feta (page 90)

Tipsy Buttered Baileys Peach Cobbler (page 245)

Netflix-and-Chill Night

Agave-Lemon Pepper Wingz (page 68)

Cereal-Crusted Buffalo Chicken Tenders (page 61)

Mango Jerk Jackfruit Tacos (page 138)

My Favorite Salted Caramel Chocolate Chip Cookies (page 214)

Completing an Exercise Streak

Crispy AF Air Fryer Green Tomatoes (page 55)

Vegan Red Beans and Rice (page 141)

Duck Fat Brussels Sprouts and Pears (page 127)

Banana Pudding Smoothie Bowl (page 47—a nice light dessert)

Dinner with Your Boo Thang

"Need a Hug" Sweet Potato Soup with Seared Scallops (page 99)

Whiskey and Sweet Tea Glazed Salmon (page 162)

Mixed-Up Potato Gratin (page 119)

Bananas Foster Tarte Tatin (page 221)

Grown Folks' Half-Birthday Brunch Celebration

Jammin' Frittata (page 36)

Gooey Baked Cheesy Grits (page 112)

Orange-Lavender Popovers (page 40)

Peach Bellini Brunch Cake (page 33—throw a candle on it!)

Treat Yo' Self Day

Winter Salad (page 93)

Harissa Chicken Chickpea Stew (page 199)

Honeychile Brown Butter Cornbread (page 115)

Salted Butterscotch Apple Whiskey Snacking Cake (page 239)

Getting a Promotion

Peri-Peri Ginger Beer Chicken (page 200)

Elote Fried Corn Pudding (page 116)

Pineapple Upside-Down Punch Bowl Cake (page 208)

Christmas in July
(sometimes life needs you to put up that Christmas tree early!)

Tamarind and Hot Honey Glazed Turkey (page 203)

Rose's Cornbread Dressing (page 121)

THE Ultimate Mac and Cheese (page 108)

Mama's Collards (page 128)

Fantasy Vacay Day

Jerk Salmon Croquettes (page 75)

Mango Jerk Jackfruit Tacos (page 138)

Caribbean Crab-Stuffed Snapper with Ginger-Lime Sauce (page 150)

Plantain Beignets with Coconut-Rum Sauce (page 231)

Impromptu Homie Gathering Nibbles

Easy Pretzel Monkey Bread with Beer-Cheese Dip (page 52)

Tempura-Fried Pickled Okra (page 81)

Crispy Greek Lemon Potato Wedges (page 111)

Maple–Brown Butter Pancetta Popcorn (page 67)

acknowledgments

Thank you, God, for the blessings of my abundance, inspired purpose, and absolute joy of doing what I truly love each and every day. I wake up feeling so blessed and full.

To my muses, Big Mama and my mama, thank you for passing so much wisdom, love, and great food to me that I now get to pass to Harmony and you.

To my daddy, thank you for being my hero and always believing in my dreams.

To my husband, Frederick, thank you for being the best friend I've ever had and the most honest recipe-testing truth-teller.

To my big brother, I'm so glad I get to annoy you with all my crazy recipe ideas and homemade songs! You mean the world to me.

To Big Daddy, thank you for being such an amazing presence in my life. You still inspire me every day.

To Auntie Rose and BB, thank you for sharing so much of your love of life and food with me.

To Jennifer Sit, the most amazing editor who truly made sure this book reached its full potential, I'm so grateful.

Thank you Brandi Bowles, the best literary agent in the world. You have been with me from the beginning. I appreciate you more than you know.

To my coauthor, Olga Massov, I literally could not have done this without you. Thank you for taking this journey with me.

To Kenneth Temple, my recipe-testing machine, thank you for helping me crank out so many ideas and helping to get them so right.

To the best photography team: Brittany, D'mytrek, Mercedes, Maeve, Dorie, and Brittany. I am so grateful for your creativity, vibrancy, and artistry on each page of this book. Thank you for breathing life into it. Thank you Rachel, Jamie, and LaMonica for making me look like a goddess on each and every page. Thank you Meiko, for keeping me all the way together my friend!

To Noah, my manager and ride-or-die. No one believes in me more than you. I can't thank you enough for always building me up.

Thank you to my business coach, Kassandra, for reminding me of my worth and potential.

To Kelly, my publicist. You see the vision when no one else does. You are such a wonderful friend and sister to me.

To my in-laws, thank you so much for your consistent love and support.

Thank you to Aunt Beverly, cousin Johnnie Mae, and to Aunt Henrietta in heaven for allowing me to share pieces of you in this book.

Thank you to my Sorors of Alpha Kappa Alpha Sorority, Inc., for your love and sisterhood.

And to my blogger boos, thank you for inspiring me in this industry and keeping me going when I'm totally burnt out. Your retreats have been my lifeline. I'm working on more choreography to teach you.

And to besties Leslie, Alesha, Tisa, and my bestie cuzes Ros and BJ, I adore you all.

Finally, thank you to all the followers, subscribers, and anyone who has ever cooked or baked one of my recipes. It has truly made my life so abundant.

Index

Note: Page references in *italics* indicate photographs.

ClarksonPotter.com
RandomHouseBooks.com

CLARKSON POTTER is a trademark and
POTTER with colophon is a registered
trademark of Penguin Random House LLC.

Library of Congress Cataloging-in-Publication Data
has been applied for.

ISBN 978-0-593-23621-5
Ebook ISBN 978-0-593-23622-2

Printed in China

Photographer: Brittany Conerly
Food Stylist: D'mytrek Brown
Food Stylist Assistants: Dori Towns,
Mercedes Evans, Brittany Neisen
Prop Stylist: Maeve Sheridan
Editor: Jennifer Sit
Editorial Assistant: Bianca Cruz
Production Editor: Joyce Wong
Production Manager: Jessica Heim
Compositors: Merri Ann Morrell and Zoe Tokushige
Copy Editor: Ivy McFadden
Indexer: Elizabeth Parson
Marketer: Stephanie Davis
Publicist: Erica Gelbard

Cover photographs by Brittany Conerly

10 9 8 7 6 5 4 3 2 1

First Edition